When Play Isn't Easy

Helping Children Enter and Sustain Play

SANDRA HEIDEMANN and DEBORAH HEWITT

Name:_____

Date:_____

Redleaf Press®
www.redleafpress.org
800-423-8309

Also from Redleaf Press by Sandra Heidemann and Deborah Hewitt:

When Play Isn't Fun: Helping Children Resolve Play Conflicts

Play: The Pathway from Theory to Practice, revised edition of *Pathways to Play*

From Deborah Hewitt:

So This Is Normal Too?, second edition

Published by Redleaf Press
10 Yorkton Court
St. Paul, MN 55117
www.redleafpress.org

First edition 2014
Cover design by Erin New
Cover photographs by Steve Wewerka
Interior design by Erin New
Typeset in Adobe Garamond Pro and Futura
Printed in the United States of America

Library of Congress Cataloging-in-Publication Data
Heidemann, Sandra, 1946-
  When play isn't easy : helping children enter and sustain play / Sandra Heidemann, Deborah Hewitt.
     pages cm
  Summary: "When children have difficulty joining play or participating in group play, it's important to pinpoint the challenges that are occurring. This book focuses on the reasons why play might not be easy for children—due to language delays, shyness, special needs, or trauma, for example—and provides specific language and activities to facilitate play and help children improve their play skills" — Provided by publisher.
  ISBN 978-1-60554-307-9 (paperback)
  1. Play—Psychological aspects. 2. Education, Preschool. 3. Child psychology.
4. Child development.   I. Hewitt, Debbie, 1958- II. Title.
  LB1139.35.P55H45 2014
  303.3'2—dc23
                         2013044404

Printed on acid-free paper   U20-09

Contents

Dear Reader,

This book and its companion reflect a renewed interest in play and how very important it is in the healthy development of children. In this new world of technology, play continues to be the most powerful force for learning in a young child's life. And our job as people who teach young children is to provide the best environment for play to happen. The first book, *When Play Isn't Fun: Helping Children Resolve Play Conflicts*, focuses on setting up your environment, schedule, and curriculum for play and highlights several group-play challenges and how to address them. This book, *When Play Isn't Easy: Helping Children Enter and Sustain Play*, offers a detailed look at the Play Checklist introduced in our book *Play: The Pathway from Theory to Practice*, plus an exploration of how play connects to early learning standards. The books build on information from *Play* and can be an additional resource to it. The books move from designing your learning environment to maximize play, to helping groups of children resolve barriers to more productive play, to helping individual children learn better play skills. The books could be used on your own, with your teaching team, or by your organization. They could be the basis of workshops.

As we began these books, we decided to ask friends and family about their experiences with play. Their memories are touching, funny, and poignant. Many of their quotes are included in the books.

Those of us who care for children have many possible roles: teacher, assistant teacher, aide, family child care provider, specialist, and others. We all interact with children as they play. We have chosen to use the term *teacher* when referring to all adults working in our field. We are all teachers in each of our roles. The suggestions are valuable whatever your title.

We have used the term *learning environment* to refer to the variety of settings we see in early childhood.

We hope these books help you to remember your own play experiences and use those memories to strengthen the play experiences for the children in your care. As you increase your intentionality with regard to play in your learning environment, children will show you their delight in new and fascinating ways.

Sandy & Debbie

Introduction

The companion to this book, *When Play Isn't Fun*, discusses how to set up your environment and plan activities for play. It also explores several group-play challenges children encounter and how you can help children solve them. This book, *When Play Isn't Easy*, also looks at play challenges but through the experience of the individual child. The book begins by outlining how play meets standards and helps you articulate your beliefs about the value of play. It moves to discussing the Play Checklist, which helps you identify what the child is doing in play. If you have children in your learning environment who experience difficulties during play, this book can help you identify problems and write goals to support children as they try out new play skills.

Time to Reflect

Sometimes individual children show us troublesome behaviors during play. Describe one child's behavior that bugs you when the child is playing with others.

_____

_____

Why do you think the behavior bothers you?

_____

_____

Looking at Your Role

Before children even enter your learning environment, you prepare by designing the space to play in, providing props related to a theme, and setting aside enough time in your schedule so children have an extended playtime. Once you have set the stage, it is time for the children to become involved in play. Your involvement isn't done, however. You continue to have a role in observing play and documenting children's skill development and because children sometimes need help:

- finding props for the play.
- solving conflicts.
- joining play.
- sustaining play.

At times teachers use the free-choice time as an opportunity to take a break, finish a project, or prepare. It is easy to disengage with the children when they are happily playing. But your role as a teacher continues even then. Following are some reasons teachers don't interact with children during play:

Adults don't know what to do. Adults don't understand how play skills develop and don't know what to do to encourage more and deeper play.

Adults believe that play is not as valuable as other activities. Adults see play as something to fill time for children and don't see the learning that takes place.

Adults emphasize early literacy and math separately from play. Adults don't see how to integrate literacy and math into play. They think math and literacy need to be taught with direct, adult-led activities.

Adults believe children will play naturally and don't need adult help. Adults may remember play as older children or in settings outside of a classroom.

Adults use the time children are playing to do other chores. Adults will complete tasks such as taking attendance, preparing for groups, preparing for snack, and cleaning up rather than engaging with children during play.

Adults worry they will interfere with and interrupt children's play, perhaps harming them. Adults have absorbed the traditional view of play that adults should not be part of play experience and that if they are, they could hamper the children's participation.

It is true that children don't need adults to be with them all the time while they play and sometimes adults can even get in the way. However, you provide valuable support to children who are struggling to learn play skills. They need you to observe carefully during play, identify where their struggles and strengths are, and offer strategies to help them improve their play skills. This book is designed to help you give that support.

Time to Reflect

What do you see adults doing while children are playing? Why do you think this is so?

_____

_____

_____

_____

SELF-ASSESSMENT

The following self-assessment is intended to help you reflect on what you know about children's individual play skill development, how you analyze and plan from your observations, and how you choose strategies and a role for yourself while supporting a child learning play skills. The self-assessment reflects your understanding at this time, but you will learn more about each item as you cover the indicated chapter.

1 When I observe a child at play, I can determine how the child's play connects to early learning standards. (chapter 1)

    a) Always   b) Usually   c) Sometimes   d) Never

2 When a parent or coworker questions the value of play, I know how to respond. (chapter 2)

    a) Always   b) Usually   c) Sometimes   d) Never

3 I reflect on the ways play has changed for children and find ways to keep it fresh for them. (chapter 3)

    a) Always   b) Usually   c) Sometimes   d) Never

4 I wonder about children's play experiences outside of the classroom and how those affect them. (chapter 4)

    a) Always   b) Usually   c) Sometimes   d) Never

5 When a child isn't playing with others, I observe closely to learn why. (chapter 4)

    a) Always   b) Usually   c) Sometimes   d) Never

6 When I observe a child having difficulty with play skills, I write down my observations and reflect on them. (chapter 5)

    a) Always   b) Usually   c) Sometimes   d) Never

7 When a child isn't speaking during play, I sit near the child and encourage the child to speak to her peers. (chapter 5)

a) Always b) Usually c) Sometimes d) Never

8 I add a sensorimotor activity to dramatic play if I have a child who has a very short attention span. (chapter 5)

a) Always b) Usually c) Sometimes d) Never

9 I help the child who uses force to enter a play group learn new ways to join the group. (chapter 5)

a) Always b) Usually c) Sometimes d) Never

10 I encourage children to notice the distress of others and offer assistance. (chapter 5)

a) Always b) Usually c) Sometimes d) Never

11 When a child is having difficulty during play, I make a plan to help him. (chapter 6)

a) Always b) Usually c) Sometimes d) Never

12 I plan what role I will use when helping a child learn play skills. (chapter 7)

a) Always b) Usually c) Sometimes d) Never

13 After implementing a plan to help strengthen a child's play skills, I observe to determine if the plan is working. (chapter 8)

a) Always b) Usually c) Sometimes d) Never

Your self-assessment is a snapshot of what you know about how children develop play skills and ways you can support them. Your responses can point to areas you want to strengthen.

Time to Reflect

What did you learn about yourself from this self-assessment?

_____

_____

_____

_____

What further questions do you have after completing this self-assessment?

_____

_____

_____

_____

Using This Book

This book is divided into eight chapters. Chapter 1 explores how play connects to standards. Chapter 2 asks you to reflect on the value of play and how you communicate that value to others. Chapter 3 uncovers the kinds of connections children make through play and shares reflections on the ways play has changed. Chapter 4 describes possible reasons children have difficulty in play, which can range from language differences to special needs. Chapter 5 delves into the ten sections of the Play Checklist. It takes you through each section of the checklist step-by-step. Chapters 6 and 7 help you analyze the results of the Play Checklist, write goals, choose strategies connected to the goal, and define a role for yourself during play with an individual child who is struggling with play skills. Chapter 8 provides an opportunity to reflect on your plans and strategies.

By examining how play fulfills early learning standards and practicing responses to questions about the value of play, you will be more able to help parents, colleagues, and funders support play in your setting. When you complete this book, you will understand how developmental challenges affect children's play skills, identify where a child is having problems, and form goals and a plan for the child. Finally, you will learn to step back and evaluate the plan to see if it is working. You will continue developing your skills as you go through these steps for children in your group again and again. Supporting children as they learn new play skills is part of becoming an intentional teacher.

This book is designed to be interactive and is meant to encourage thought, reflection, and discussion. As you reflect on and then plan and implement new play strategies, you become a more intentional teacher providing children with rich play experiences.

CHAPTER 1 **Learning from Play**

Children eagerly seek out play experiences. They are excited about new toys and ask repeatedly to play certain games. They seek out friends to play house, doctor, fire department, or shopping. When adults develop and write standards that focus on the many developmental gains children make in their earliest years, or when they are teaching children with attention to the standards, they may minimize or miss the powerful learning that happens in the hearts and minds of children as they play. Perhaps you have heard adults state with some amusement, "Oh, they are *just* playing." This statement trivializes children's experiences and dismisses how play inspires, challenges, and changes children. Play is key to young children's development and is the one of the most influential ways they learn.

> When I was in preschool, it was fun when it was recess and I was almost done
> with monkey bars—when I was almost able to do them all without falling.
> —Johann, age 6

Content in this chapter connects with chapter 1 in *Play: The Pathway from Theory to Practice.*

Skills Children Learn through Play

When adults first think of what children are learning in play, they think of social skills or learning to share. Children acquire these skills in play, and they learn so much more. Here are some additional ways in which play benefits children:

- Children learn how to speak and listen.
- Children learn how to make and keep friends.
- Children learn how to imagine.
- Children learn how to plan ahead.
- Children learn how to tell a story.
- Children learn how to imagine with objects and props.
- Children learn how to take turns.
- Children learn how to join in.
- Children learn how to use literacy and math in the real world.

- Children learn how to take risks.
- Children learn how to build on interests.

Time to Reflect

What do you think children learn through play?

_____

_____

_____

_____

I remember dancing in the basement to Herb Alpert and "The Pink Panther."
I spent hours making up new moves to perform over the furniture, across the
floor, and through the doorways. —Becky

Connecting Standards to Play

More than likely, your state has a set of early learning standards that guide your
work with young children. These standards typically address cognitive, physical,
language, and socioemotional development. The standards outline what young
children are learning in each of these domains. However, clearly identifying these
domains in your learning environment can be challenging. As you think about
how children are meeting standards in your environment, remember that play
helps children learn and develop skills in each of these domains.

Time to Reflect

Think about your learning environment and answer the following questions:

Cognitive: Which play activities challenge children's thinking?

_____

_____

_____

_____

Physical: Which play activities encourage children to move their large and small muscles?

_____

_____

_____

_____

Language: How do you see children speaking, listening, and communicating in play?

_____

_____

_____

_____

Socioemotional: How do you see children expressing their emotions, understanding others' emotions, and regulating their feelings during play?

_____

_____

_____

_____

Connecting Play to Standards

Another way to understand how play experiences connect to children's learning is to start with the experience and connect the experience to the standards. Following is an example of a bulletin board one staff developed to illustrate how much children learn through play. Underneath the play experience, list what children are learning. The learning will probably involve more than one domain.

Family Bulletin Board

When children play in the sand, they are learning to:

When children play in the house area, they are learning to:

When children play in the block area, they are learning to:

When children climb on the jungle gym, they are learning to:

Engaging the Whole Child

Play engages the whole child. When children run and jump, they stimulate their muscles and their brains. As children gain in their language abilities, they are more able to solve their conflicts with words. This is what we mean when we emphasize working with the whole child. Although standards are divided into different domains, always remember that no child is divided into parts. Play helps us provide motivating and engaging activities that give children a developmental boost in all areas. Play gives children opportunities to meet these standards.

As you deepen your understanding of your state's early learning standards, you will see children reaching those standards again and again through play. Your close documentation of the improvements in children's skills through play will give you relevant material to share with parents and your colleagues. You help children use play as a vehicle to accomplish the standards by setting up a rich environment, scaffolding the play both of groups of children and individual children who are not able to participate fully in play, and implementing plans that support all children as they explore through play.

Time to Reflect

Observe a child during play for a few minutes. What do you see the child doing? What was the child playing with? What do you think the child was learning?

_____

_____

_____

_____

Where do you see children most engaged in play? Is it outdoors? Is it in certain play areas in your learning environment? What do you see them doing?

_____

_____

_____

_____

Sharing the Value of Play

When you affirm that play is important to a child's development, families, funders, colleagues, and even directors or principals may not agree and may challenge your decisions about curriculum, daily schedules, or expenditures. Some of these reactions are based on mistaken ideas and beliefs about play. Adults often miss how children learn through play. Practicing and preparing responses to these reactions gives you tools to answer their reservations. You may get questions from the following individuals:

Families. Families are anxious about preparing their children for school. They want to make sure that what you do will help their children.

Funders. Funding can come from foundations, counties, cities, or the federal government. These parties are very concerned about outcomes and results and may question play's value in helping children reach those outcomes.

Colleagues. Other teachers, providers, or staff may question how much time should be reserved for play.

Directors or principals. Directors or principals may not have received training in early childhood and lack understanding of how play fits into a child's development.

> Content in this chapter connects with chapter 1 in *Play: The Pathway from Theory to Practice.*

Time to Reflect

The discussion above may remind you of statements you have heard about play. List statements, positive or negative, you have heard about play and young children.

_____

_____

_____

_____

I also remember in our preschool we all brought a stuffed animal in. We left the stuffed animals to spend the night and have a sleepover. When we got back the next day, our preschool classroom was TRASHED—shaving cream on mirrors, toilet paper everywhere, toys out of place. We were told that our stuffed animals got a little out of hand. It was magical to think they all were playing in the night while we sang the cleanup song the next day and took care of the mess. —Lisa C.

What Would You Say?

As professionals and advocates for children, we must be ready to educate others about the value of play. When others challenge us, it is easy to become upset, anxious, and resentful. We may respond in a dismissive manner. Learning how to respond in an effective way requires you to think ahead and practice.

Here are some of the questions you might hear:

- Are they just playing?

- What are they learning anyway?

- Do you just let them play all day?

- How will we have time for math and literacy groups if we let them play?

It is hard to find answers to these questions if you are feeling vulnerable and unsure. Thinking ahead and practicing prepares you to respond before you are put on the spot. Following is an example of how one teacher answered a question about how play connects to standards.

☀ Lauren was tense and little nervous. A group of prospective families was visiting her classroom and she wanted to show them her best. After they had observed the children during free-choice time and watched her large-group time, one of the mothers asked, "I just read about the early learning standards, especially the ones around early math and literacy. I didn't see you doing anything like that this morning." Lauren took a deep breath and said, "I'd really like to show you how I meet the early learning standards in my learning areas. Why don't you come with me and I will show you?" Lauren took the families around and pointed out the many ways children were meeting the standards as they played.

Following are a few examples for you to read and then decide how you would reply. There is not one right way to answer these questions, so take some time to think about how you would respond.

☀ Marian greeted two parents who came to see her family child care home before they enrolled their two children. She was happy they came during free-choice time, when they could see the children playing throughout the room.

However, they frowned slightly as she explained the curriculum that had emphasis on play. The mother said, "But they are just playing. When are you doing learning activities? We would like to see those."

Time to Reflect

How would you respond?

_____

_____

_____

_____

Matt's program had just gotten a grant to do literacy with the children, and he knew several visitors were coming that day from the county to observe the program. He made sure the dramatic play area had literacy props such as pencils, clipboards, signs, and menus for the restaurant. He was excited that the visitors would see how the children played with the props. After the visitors observed his large group, the children ran to the various interest areas to play. Several children gathered at the restaurant. Some put on aprons and pretended to cook. A couple of children sat down and read the menus. One of the visitors looked at the children and said, "What are they learning, anyway, when they do this restaurant?"

Time to Reflect

How would you respond?

_____

_____

_____

_____

Nadia worked hard to clean her classroom because the director was going to observe her that morning. She posted her lesson plans and daily schedule. She set up her dramatic play area to reflect her current theme: transportation. She built a train in the block area and moved the house area a little so that there was a waiting room for the train station. She put up transportation signs throughout the areas. The director was late coming in the room so missed her large group and most of the small groups. When the director entered, children were going to the interest areas and many of them were excited to play train. The director watched a few minutes and then left the room to deal with another pressing matter. Nadia met with the director later and the director asked her, "Do you just let them play all day?"

Time to Reflect

How would you respond?

_____

_____

_____

_____

Kim and Teresa were team teaching for the first time in a Head Start program. They had just sat down to write out their daily schedule. The half-day schedule was packed. They had to serve the children breakfast and lunch, do large and small groups, and schedule toothbrushing after every meal. Kim wrote down forty minutes for play and Teresa objected, "We can't let them play that long. We have too much to do. We have to do math and literacy and go outside. And then we have lunch. We have to cut it down to twenty minutes."

Time to Reflect

How would you respond?

_____

_____

_____

_____

What about Parents?

Parents are worried about their children's progress. They may become critical of the amount of time you schedule for play in your day. Underneath those critical words, however, are concerns that parents feel deeply. They may have concerns about their children and their own adequacy as parents. They may be worried about how their child will do in elementary school. They may have had painful experiences themselves in school and don't want their children to repeat them. They may be hearing from other parents, family members, or friends what young children should be learning and how they should be learning it. They may have read repeatedly that children need to succeed in school to succeed in life.

Time to Reflect

When you speak with parents about their children, what are you hearing? What feelings are underneath the words?

_____

_____

_____

_____

How do you feel when parents question your decisions about teaching?

_____

_____

_____

_____

Responding to Parent Concerns

To effectively talk about how children learn through play, it is important to understand what parents are feeling and why they are asking about what their children are learning when they play. You may feel defensive or impatient when they question you. Perhaps you feel they don't trust you, but more likely than not, they are just worried and need your reassurance and listening ear. Here are some suggestions to help you discuss how you see play:

- Spend time with parents just listening to their concerns. Try to listen first and then ask questions about their worries.

- Share examples of what you have seen their child doing during play.

- Ask parents to observe their child with you as they play and point out what the child is learning as he or she plays.

- Share an article or handout on play that outlines its value for young children.

- During conferences, point out the child's growth and how play contributed to it.

- Write a philosophy of play and its value for young children that you can share with parents. If you work in a center, share it with your director and other staff. It could evolve into a statement about your program's curriculum and philosophy.

Once parents understand how play promotes children's learning, they can set up play in their homes that further children's goals.

Learn how to communicate your belief in the value of play with parents, funders, colleagues, and administrators. When you are questioned about why you provide many opportunities for play in your learning environment and you give well-thought-out responses, you are advocating for the children in your group.

Time to Reflect

Write a short statement on the value of play. Choose someone to share it with.

_____

_____

_____

_____

Draw a picture or design that expresses how you remember feeling when you were playing as a young child.

Write a wish for how the children in your care will experience play.

_____

_____

_____

_____

The Play Surveys and Connections through Play

Learning is about the connections children make as they explore their environment, listen to stories, and participate in discussions. Children learn by making connections between what they hear and see and what they think. Children make connections when they connect an amount with a number. They are making connections when they learn to recognize the letters from their names and understand that those letters in the right order are their names. These connections help children remember words, numbers, and how things work. One day while I (Sandy) was observing a classroom, a teacher was introducing the concept of circulation. One child listened to the word and then excitedly exclaimed, "It sounds like circle." The child had made an important connection and will better remember how circulation works in the body because it goes in a circle.

Play is also about connections. Children make connections when they learn to pretend with objects. They connect what they know about an object and how it is used with another object. Children make connections between what they see adults do in their daily lives and what they play in their pretend roles. The most important connections children make in play are with each other. Think of the excitement children express when they find a new friend to play with. Think of how sad children are when connections are broken through conflicts and misunderstandings. When you provide a learning environment filled with playful opportunities, you are helping children make connections with others. When you help an individual child learn to make a connection, even if for a short time, you are enriching that's child's life. Connections are why play is important.

Time to Reflect

Describe a time when you watched a child learn something new. How did the child respond? What did you feel?

_____

_____

_____

_____

The Play Surveys

When we started this book and the companion book, *When Play Isn't Fun*, we decided to ask friends, family, and colleagues to fill out a play survey. As the surveys came back, we realized their play stories added real life stories about play. The respondents, ranging in age from six years to eighty-six years, shared stories about their fun, conflicts, toys, and playmates. Their stories appear in many places in the books to illustrate our points. In this chapter, we look a little more deeply at their answers. First, we use their stories to demonstrate vividly the connections children make during play. Second, we share information from the surveys that surprised us and caused us to reflect further on some of our own questions about play.

Play Connections

The play survey respondents answered questions about special toys they played with, friends or groups of friends they sought out, and places they played. The answers varied greatly and depended on where they grew up as children, how big their family was, and what they observed adults doing around them. Although the context of their play experiences varied, they all had made connections during play that mirror the kinds of connections children make today. The connections can be broken down into four main categories:

- connections to others
- connections to place
- connections to toys and objects
- connections to adults and their roles

Connections to Others

Children who grow up in large families rarely play alone, while children in small families or only children often play alone. Children have friends in the neighborhood and friends from school with shared interests. Children in early childhood settings connect to their peers and make friends as they learn to play together.

> I mostly played alone, as I was an "only" child for the first four years of my life. I played with my "imaginary friends"; for example, outside I'd push the empty swing and talk away to the swing. Or I'd set my little table and chairs with doll dishes for lunch with my imaginary friends. —Linda D.

> I had a special friend my age and really enjoyed playing at her house and began to feel almost a part of her family as well. We would play *Man from U.N.C.L.E.* (a television program at that time) for hours at a time in the small woods behind our house. She moved several miles away in grade school, but her mom started a sewing group for us and we would go to her house about once a week and do simple needlework. —Gera

Connections to Place

Urban and rural settings elicit different kinds of play behaviors and friendships. In a rural setting, children may have more access to nature and weave those themes and materials into their play. They may be more isolated and often play alone, unless they come from a large family. Children in urban or suburban settings may play in their neighborhoods, in streets, in parks, and in community centers, or be taken by their parents to play groups. You also provide a special place for play in your indoor and outdoor settings. Some children prefer to play outside, and when you provide dramatic play outside, their play deepens and expands.

> At my parents' farm, I had a Shetland pony named Pickles that I could ride every day when my dad got home from work. I also used to tie all of his hunting duck decoys together and drag them around the yard as pets. My brother and I would help with the chores, and we loved our horses. —Sarah

> There was a group of kids roughly the same age who all played together. It varied each day depending on who was allowed out and who was being punished for something. We flipped baseball cards, rode bikes, and played football and street baseball. —Jim G.

Connections to Toys and Objects

Children tend to play with objects and materials available to them. If they grow up in settings with natural materials available, children may pretend the rocks are animals and a concoction of mud and water baked in the sun is a big cake. In an urban or suburban setting, children may spend less time outside and more time playing with toys inside. Children can become very attached to the objects they play with. Children cherish certain dolls, and they drive the same cars and trucks over and over. Children insist on bringing their stuffed animals to bed with them. Even in your setting children become very attached to certain toys and objects. Some of them are so popular, children fight to play with them.

> About the only thing I remember from my early childhood was a straw cowboy hat and toy pistol and holster, which I would wear as I rode my imaginary steed around our house on adventures in which I starred as a cowboy hero. —Steve M.

> I did have a special baby doll that my mom bought me. I had never had one and against her better judgment she got one for me, even though she thought I was too old. She got me a cradle for it and I just loved her! I dressed her, fed her, rocked her, and cradled her. I named her "Katie"—the name of one of my daughters today. Still a fond memory. —Gera

Connections to Adults and Their Roles

Children reflect what they see adults doing in their homes, schools, and communities. Children pretend to be mothers, fathers, doctors, nurses, police officers, and firefighters. Children often imitate roles they see on television or in the movies. You may even see children playing school in your setting, and as you watch the "teacher" you may wonder if you really sound like that when you are reading a story. Although children may not act out a role exactly as you see it, they are reflecting back to adults what they understand about the role: what the person does and says.

> As a young child, my favorite experience was outside swinging and singing or playing in the sandbox. I also enjoyed pretending, role-playing the adult roles I observed in my life like playing house, store clerk, postal worker, or Sunday school teacher. —Linda D.

Time to Reflect

Think about connections you made during play as a child. Describe one of those connections. It could be a connection to a place, object, person, or adult role.

_____

_____

_____

_____

Surprising Themes

Some of the answers to the surveys were surprising to us. We have often thought about the prevalence of violence in children's play and have wondered if play is more violent now. We have heard teachers in workshops express concern over the amount and intensity of violence in children's play based on what they see on television and in movies and video games. They describe children's play as more imitative and less imaginative. Throughout the surveys, adults also recounted stories of physical conflicts and disagreements during play, some resulting in injuries. Several respondents described play themes like cops and robbers that can develop into violent interactions.

> We played cops and robbers or good guys/bad guys. This was because of my brothers. —Kim

Survey respondents wrote about play that started out as fun and then became excessively physical, resulting in injuries or hurt feelings. This play often involved throwing things at each other, such as rocks or sticks, or punching each other in jest. Sometimes these punches were thrown to solve conflicts, but sometimes such behavior was a way to connect with each other.

> My cousin Karen said mean things to me about my dad. I punched her. End of story. —Claire

> *Guerritas* (little wars) is another game we played. With a rubber band we would launch cactus plants at each other. —Edgar

> I can't recall anything serious, other than the chestnut fight I got into with Jackie at about age six. We had a big chestnut tree in our yard. Jackie substituted a rock for a chestnut, which hit me in the mouth, chipping a tooth. —Steve M.

Conflict in Play

The adults and children who filled out the play survey also shared stories of conflicts that involved fighting, punching, or throwing things. These behaviors often resulted in injuries and/or disruptions in relationships. Adults remember experiencing strong feelings when having conflicts as children. They were angry, upset, and sometimes defiant. Over and over again respondents wrote that they solved their own conflicts without the intervention of an adult. And the way to solve them involved violence. When adults did become involved, it was often after an injury.

> We had two neighborhoods that had differences over territory for riding our bikes. We settled this dispute in a twenty-minute rock throwing fight where I received my first stitches after being hit in the head with a rock. This, of course, raised my status with the older kids and my peers. I took one for our street/ neighborhood. —Jim G.

> Conflicts were usually solved by boxing or wrestling. I don't recall ever taking them to an adult. —Maynard

Our questions about play and violence are difficult to answer. Perhaps children's play has always included fighting, disagreements, and physical conflicts. It also may be true that children's play now reflects the more violent themes they see through video games, television, and movies. But these stories do remind us that children will fight, disagree, and tussle as they play together. And because they don't always have the judgment or impulse control, they may do things out of exuberance or anger that hurt others or themselves, especially when out of the presence of adults. You have an opportunity in your learning environment to help children learn to express their anger through words and learn to stop themselves before they hurt a peer. You can demonstrate how you solve problems and can teach children the problem-solving steps. It is difficult to know if children play more violently now or have more conflicts. The respondents' stories, however, resonate with children's experiences in many early childhood settings.

Children make connections to other people, to beloved objects and places, and to adult roles they have seen around them when they play. These connections deepen and enhance their learning. When the connections during play are broken through conflict, trauma, or developmental delays, children's play is affected. The next chapter explores in more depth why these connections during play can be difficult for children. Whatever the reasons, your role is to help children make the profound connections to others that play can bring.

Time to Reflect

Do you think children play more violently now than you did when you were a child? Why or why not?

_____

_____

_____

_____

How do you think children's play has changed since you were a child? What seems to be the same?

_____

_____

_____

_____

Understanding Play Difficulties  CHAPTER 4

Children often have difficulty while playing together. It may be hard to fit in or get along with other children. It may not be easy to share a desired toy. Some of these difficulties are temporary or short-term. When children are ill or experiencing changes in their lives, they may be tired, cry easily, and become upset if things don't go their way. But when they feel better or things at home settle down, they recover their ability to play with others and get along. Some children, however, frequently show stress or anxiety when playing with their peers. They need more help from adults to learn to problem solve, take turns, or pretend a role.

Time to Reflect

Describe a child in your care who consistently is not able to play well with others. What behaviors are you seeing? How do you feel about the child?

_____

_____

_____

_____

> Content in this chapter connects with chapter 4 in *Play: The Pathway from Theory to Practice.*

Influences on Play Difficulties

Children bring their whole selves when they play. Therefore, when children are experiencing trauma or developmental delays, their play skills are influenced. How their play skills are affected differs with each particular challenge. Because each child is unique you may see a variety of reactions to similar experiences. Although it is impossible to predict each child's reaction to these challenges, the following are several challenges that influence children's play:

Culture. Children who do not share a similar cultural identification may experience confusion when playing. They may have different experiences of what adults cook with, ways adults communicate, and gender roles. They may not be able to play roles that match the experiences of other children in the group. They may leave out children who do not share their experiences.

Differences in home languages. It is harder for children to verbally create play story scenarios or develop roles in play when they do not share a language. Like children with cultural differences, children who do not speak the group's dominant language may be left out themselves or leave out other children.

Gender. Boys and girls may choose different play areas and toys. They may want to play different play themes and may exclude children of the opposite gender. Young children are just beginning to incorporate gender identity and can be quite convinced they know where boys and girls belong and what they should be doing. Sometimes children simply avoid areas because they see them as "girl" areas or "boy" areas, such as only boys play in the block area and only girls play in the house area. Other times they try to stop children of the opposite gender from joining the group play.

Temperament. Children are born with temperaments that shape their initial reactions to situations. Children who are very shy may find it hard to join a group; children who are active may find it hard to stay with a play theme and may move around play areas quickly.

Lack of experience with props or theme. Sometimes when children don't engage with props or join in a dramatic play theme, they lack experience with them. Some children don't have many toys in their homes or are unfamiliar with the toys included in your environment. Some dramatic play themes may be so specific and even unfamiliar that children don't understand the roles or scenarios they can create.

Exposure to trauma. When children have been stressed by traumatic experiences, their play skills can be affected. They may become very withdrawn and refuse to play with other children, aggressive toward others, especially in conflicts over toys, and prone to react dramatically when things don't go their way. For example, children may scream and cry if they don't get to play the role they want or if other children won't cooperate regarding the play scenario. Trauma can range from serious and ongoing stress, such as violence in the home or neighborhood, to the more temporary stress of moving. Possible adverse childhood experiences are separation and divorce, death of a close loved one, parental depression or mental illness, and homelessness.

Special needs. Special needs such as autism, language delays, and behavior challenges all affect a child's play, especially with others. Sometimes a child demonstrates problematic behaviors without having a diagnosis. In these cases, observe and address the behaviors without putting a label on the child. However, if a child has a diagnosis, you may be able to anticipate some of the play challenges. Autism affects a child's desire and ability to interact in a group. Language delays affect children's abilities to communicate and often result in behavioral aggression because they can't express their needs or feelings. Behavior challenges such as defiance or poor impulse control make it tough for a child to cooperate in a group-play situation.

☀ Soren flew into the classroom with a frown on his face. His mother followed him, shaking her head in frustration. Tonia, his teacher, approached him gingerly because she didn't want to set him off. She knew if she started the day wrong with Soren, he would be fighting with the other children all morning. Last week he had pushed down a child on the playground, and Tonia had to call both sets of parents about the incident. When she tried to discipline Soren, he just looked at her and frowned. He didn't say anything. He didn't look remorseful or sad. Soren usually had a hard time joining a group to play. He would walk into an area, hit a child, and demand to play. Tonia wasn't sure how to help him because she knew he did really want to play with other children.

You may have worked with children like Soren. Children who constantly fight with other children, don't know how to join play, hang around the fringes of the play, or are rejected by their peers can break your heart. They also challenge your patience. Yet, like Tonia, we are often unsure how to help them. Many children, like Soren, want to play with their peers but lack the skills to play in a group successfully.

Time to Reflect

Why do you think Tonia was approaching Soren so carefully?

_____

_____

_____

_____

Have you ever been in a similar situation with a child? If so, what strategies did you use so you could respond patiently to the child's behavior?

_____

_____

_____

_____

Going Deeper into Play Influences

The play influences listed above are complex and affect children in varying ways. It is impossible to predict how a child may react to these challenges. When children have development challenges, such as language delays, or traumatic experiences, such as parents divorcing, the effects on their behavior and play can vary. A child may have a special need that is relatively mild and require little assistance from adults. Another child, however, may be experiencing a similar condition and need a lot of adult support. Therefore, although it is important to understand how these different influences may affect a child's play skills, always spend time observing and understanding the individual child. Following are descriptions of three play influences in more depth.

How Temperament Affects Play

Children may display differences in activity level, adaptability, regularity, and distractibility. Some children approach a new dramatic play with curiosity; others hang back until they see how the props work and how they will fit in. The children who hang back and avoid interactions with others are often categorized as shy. When approaching new people or experiences, their hearts beat faster and their blood pressure goes up, which indicates a biological reaction to temperament differences. Children may have a basically positive or negative approach to stress and changes in their lives. When children with a more positive outlook encounter a conflict with other children, they demonstrate a readiness to compromise and negotiate; others with a more negative response fuss and cry when play doesn't go their way. These characteristics are inborn and are accentuated by the experiences children encounter in their families and neighborhoods. It doesn't mean this initial reaction can't be changed over time. However, by understanding a child's temperament, you can plan play strategies that match that tendency. If a child is active, plan a dramatic play theme that is active and outdoors. If a child is shy or slow to approach new situations and people, set up small play groups or play with just one other child.

☼ Juan's natural tendency was to seek activities that involved movement. He loved to climb, run, and slide. His friend, José, had a quieter temperament and sought out activities like building with table blocks or reading books. José chose to observe and plan ahead when given a challenge, whereas Juan would jump in and try different solutions. Petra, their teacher, was surprised they were friends because they were so different. Juan always wanted to go outside and was the first out to the playground when it was time. She wanted Juan to settle down a little, and she wanted José to run and jump without reservation when outside. She decided to plan activities they could do together and take advantage of their friendship to encourage them in new directions. One afternoon she set up an obstacle course outside and introduced it by reading *Rosie's Walk* by Pat Hutchins during group time. Rosie is a hen who goes for a walk in the farmyard. A fox is trying to follow and get Rosie. Rosie is unaware of the fox and calmly goes on her walk while the fox encounters calamity after calamity and never does catch up to Rosie. Petra asked the children to pretend they were Rosie and go through an obstacle course. She paired up José and Juan. Petra's plan gave José a chance to observe other children go through the obstacle course and plan how to get through it with Juan; it gave Juan a chance to lead them both as they went over, under, and around the obstacles.

How Language Delays Affect Play

Language is woven into play. Watch children as they play in the dramatic play area. They use language to convey what they are pretending, organize and plan their play scenarios together, and communicate in their roles. They also use language to problem solve when they encounter conflicts and disagreements. When children have language delays or disorders, they have a harder time communicating during play. Children who are English-language learners are not delayed in learning their home language but may not have the English skills to keep up and may experience similar difficulties in play. Articulation problems can prevent adults and other children from understanding children when they speak and can make those children self-conscious. Children may have language delays or disorders that either make it hard for them to process or comprehend what is said to them or that hinder their efforts to find the words to express their thoughts. Because language is so important in carrying out play, these children are at a disadvantage. You may see children with a language issue entering play through force or disruption because they don't have the words to use.

When children cannot process information easily, they may misunderstand what other children are telling them about the play scenario or their roles. If there is a conflict, that child may find it easier to hit others rather than use words to problem solve. When children cannot keep up because of language delays and use physical ways to express their displeasure, other children start to exclude them. They may express reluctance to play with them. Sometimes children with language delays will exclude themselves and not even try to interact with other children. If you have children with language delays, help them learn to enter groups without force. Give them a specific, needed prop and ask them to take it into the dramatic play area. When a child does not attempt to enter the play, sit nearby and encourage the child to play near the group or play with just one other child.

✳ Gerald heard loud voices in the block area and walked over to see what was happening. Two children, Mason and Javianna, were building an airport and had just finished a road leading up to it. Thai had come into the area and started kicking the road so that it broke apart. Mason and Javianna were yelling at Thai to stop. Gerald sat the three of them down together and asked each of them, "What is the problem?" Mason and Javianna loudly aired their complaint about the broken road, but Thai said little. Gerald knew Thai had a language delay and couldn't express himself easily. He asked Thai if he wanted to play with Mason and Javianna. Thai nodded his head. Gerald asked the three of them to think about how they all could play together in the block area. Javianna suggested that Thai could build the road again and put cars on it going to the airport. The three of them agreed and the airport play continued. The next day Gerald watched Thai carefully and stopped him before he wrecked buildings or toys. He helped him enter the group playing in the block area by bringing in a new prop.

How Trauma Affects Play

Trauma in children's lives can interrupt their developmental progress. When children are stressed by their experiences, they cannot concentrate enough to sustain learning. They may become overanxious or angry. You may see a reaction to conflicts and disappointments that seems overwrought. All children hit bumps in the road that affect them. Families experience upheaval through moves, loss of employment, or divorce. With support a child can get through these challenges. A child who overcomes adversity learns to be resilient, to get up when knocked down and start over. However, if the child experiences ongoing stress, trauma, and adverse experiences, the brain's development is changed. There is little chance to recover before the next stressful event happens. The child learns to approach learning situations with fear and distrust.

Although a child's overall development may be stunted by chronic trauma, such as abuse, parental mental illness, or parental death, the child's emotional development will, more than likely, be severely affected. The child can be overwhelmed with the feelings and reactions brought on by the trauma, especially if the child is not given opportunities to process the trauma and offered adult assistance and encouragement. These traumatic experiences affect children's play as well. They may be less likely to join in and may withdraw from groups. They may jump to defend themselves when there is no need to fight. They may have a flat affect or show little emotion even if excited. This demeanor may not attract friends or may even scare other children a little. When you help children who have experienced trauma learn more effective play skills, you give them a picture of what is possible. If children are able to suspend the many overwhelming feelings and lose themselves in play, the benefits are immeasurable.

※ Terrance and Barb are family child care providers who care for a group of ten children in their home. Jon was new to the group and they were concerned about him. He was very quiet and held back from participating in play. He didn't smile very much and, in fact, didn't show much emotion at all. They decided to talk more with Jon's mother about their concerns. His mother was not surprised to hear about Jon's behavior. She said they had just left his dad because of domestic violence. It was a new start for them, but Jon was still experiencing fear and anxiety. He was seeing a counselor to talk about his feelings. Terrance and Barb decided to support Jon so he could more easily participate. They set up activities they knew he liked, such as building with Lego blocks and Magna-Tiles. They made sure at least one other child was also included in the activities. They played next to the two children without pressuring Jon to talk or interact. It took a few weeks, but slowly Jon came out of his shell and started to communicate with them and with the other children. Terrance and Barb were very excited when Jon first smiled at another child while they were playing with playdough.

Children's play can be influenced and changed by a variety of challenges. The challenges can involve differing cultures and languages or a wide range of special needs. Temperaments affect how children react to conflicts or new play experiences. Trauma can cause such anxiety and stress that children shut down and cease communicating even during play. Special needs can alter a child's play behaviors so that it is difficult to participate in group play. Although we may not know exactly what is causing a child to lack connections to others during play or to engage in fights and conflicts, we can find ways to help individual children grow in their play skills. The next chapter focuses on an assessment aid called the Play Checklist; it will help you identify where a child has struggles and assist you in making goals and plans to support that child.

Time to Reflect

Look again at the child you wrote about at the start of this chapter. Which factors do you think are influencing this child's play?

_____

_____

_____

_____

What surprised you as you read this chapter?

_____

_____

_____

_____

What do you want to share with your colleagues or other providers?

_____

_____

_____

_____

CHAPTER 5 # Using the Play Checklist

You may not understand why many children are not able to enjoy play experiences, are left out, or behave aggressively toward other children. But you can help them learn to be more successful during play. With your help and support they can learn more effective strategies, but first you need to be able to identify where the child is having difficulty. The Play Checklist was developed to help you identify more clearly what a child is doing or not doing during play.

Content in this chapter connects with chapter 5 in *Play: The Pathway from Theory to Practice.*

Using the Play Checklist to Help Children

The Play Checklist helps you identify where a child may be struggling in play. Once you have completed the checklist, you will know the child's level and be able to plan goals to support the child's growth in play skills. All children experience times of conflict, disappointment, and hurt feelings while playing with others. However, the Play Checklist is designed to help children who are *consistently* left out, in conflicts with peers, playing alone, or unable to take turns. Although the checklist was developed for children in the preschool age range, you can also use it for younger children as long as you expect them to be functioning only at the lower levels of the checklist. You could also complete the checklist for children in kindergarten and early elementary grades. You can expect that they will be functioning at the upper levels of the checklist. If you use the checklist, you will see both where the child is having problems and a pathway to help. The Play Checklist provides the following:

- help understanding the components of sociodramatic play

- help identifying areas of concern

- help planning strategies for the child

The following sections outline the steps to using the Play Checklist: deciding whom to observe, observing the child, and completing the checklist. After reading about the steps, you will have an opportunity to practice them.

Decide Whom to Observe

Choose one child to observe. Perhaps you have already identified a child to observe. Or, it may be hard to decide because there are several children having difficulty. If you are wondering how to make the choice, refer to the following list to help you decide whether a child is in need of an observation:

- a child who consistently has trouble interacting with a small group or a particular individual
- a child who often plays alone and seems distressed by it
- a child who is flitting around play areas with little focus
- a child who is rejected when she attempts to join a group to play
- a child who becomes aggressive when playing with others
- a child who only manipulates objects rather than pretending with them
- a child who is silent or talking only to himself
- a child who refuses to take turns

As you review the list, consider the frequency and severity of any difficulty. In addition, children who show difficulty in several areas would benefit from your observation and completion of the checklist.

Observe the Child

Although it can be difficult to set aside time to observe in a busy learning environment, the information you gain helps you complete the checklist. Observe the child two or three times, for ten minutes each time, during free-choice time. Try to catch the child in the dramatic play area, where there are plenty of opportunities to pretend, act out roles, and interact with a group of children. Write a running record or anecdotal notes, which are descriptions of what you see the child doing and saying while you are observing. Keep your mind open because you may observe something you didn't expect. Sometimes your perceptions and previous experiences with children can color your interpretations of their behavior. Describe behavior and try to avoid making judgments about the child's feelings or thoughts.

Using Descriptions in Your Observations

The following are statements from teachers' observations. Decide whether the statements reflect judgments or descriptions. Write *J* for judgments and *D* for descriptions.

_____ Amy cried for twenty minutes when she first arrived today. She sat on the teacher's lap.

_____ Amy missed her mother this morning and sought out her favorite teacher. She wasn't feeling well.

_____ Derek lay down during the circle time and rolled on the floor. When asked by the teacher to sit up, he did, but started to poke the child next to him. A teacher sat near Derek and put a hand on his back. He stopped the poking.

_____ Derek wasn't interested in group today. He didn't like the book. First he lay down and then he bothered another child.

_____ Erika was very rude today. She laughed when another child fell down. Sometimes I just don't think Erika cares what others feel.

_____ Erika laughed when the child she was running with fell down. She turned around and offered the child a hand to get up.

Read the following anecdotal record:

☀ Markus was so mad today. He didn't like any of the kids in the group and wouldn't play with them. He ran around and knocked down the buildings. He was disrespectful toward the teachers. He didn't perform up to his ability because he scribbled his name for sign-in.

What is wrong with this anecdotal record?

_____

_____

_____

_____

Rewrite the record so that it more accurately describes Markus.

_____

_____

_____

_____

Finding the Time

It can be hard to pull yourself away from the bustle of your learning environment to observe one child. Here are some strategies teachers have used:

- Set up absorbing activities in other areas of the room, such as playdough or water play, so other children are involved.

- Set up a small-group situation with the child and a few other children in the dramatic play area so it is easier to observe the child. Let your teammates know you will be observing.

- Ask your teammates to help observe if you are busy.

- Arrange for teammates to be available to help other children while you are observing.

- If you are in a center, ask the director or another teacher to come in for a few minutes while you observe.

Time to Reflect

What are some strategies for observing that would work in your learning environment?

_____

_____

_____

_____

Complete the Play Checklist

Go back to your observation and use it to complete the checklist. You will find a blank Play Checklist at the back of this book that you can copy for repeated use. The checklist will help you interpret your observation and understand the components of play based on the following criteria:

- It moves from the easiest skill to the most complex.

- It looks at both play behaviors, such as pretending, and play skills, such as taking turns.

- It is developmental, as easiest items are usually done by younger children.

The checklist can be used in a number of ways. For example, some teachers decide to do the whole checklist for one child because they are concerned about the child's play skills but unsure where the child has the most difficulty. Here are other ways you can use the checklist:

- You can complete one or two sections if you know the child is struggling with those sections.

- You can complete one or two sections for your whole group of children to help you understand what you can do for group goals.

- You can complete the whole checklist or sections for a small group of children who are struggling with similar issues.

The checklist is divided into ten sections with items listed under each section heading. To complete the checklist, you check the item that matches your observation. It is okay not to be completely sure which item in each section you should check for the child. The child you observe may show different behaviors on different days. Just check the level you see the child performing most frequently.

After you complete the checklist you will be able to decide on a focus and make a plan to help the child learn more mature play skills.

Time to Reflect

Identify a child from your group who is having difficulty during play. You will observe this child to complete the checklist.

_____

What type(s) of difficulties is this child demonstrating?

_____

_____

_____

Observe the child at least two times, ten to fifteen minutes at a time. Write a running record or anecdotal notes. Use your notes to complete the checklist.

Describe any difficulties in or barriers to completing the observations.

_____

_____

_____

How did you solve them?

_____

_____

_____

The rest of the chapter focuses on the ten sections of the Play Checklist. Use your notes and observations to complete them.

1 PRETENDING WITH OBJECTS

When children play store and they don't have pretend money, they may put their hand in yours and state, "Here is a dollar." They are pretending with imaginary money. Children don't have the ability to pretend imaginary objects until they are able to understand that their gesture is representing money, usually by ages three to four. Learning to pretend requires pretending as toddlers with real objects or real-looking objects. Gradually they learn to substitute objects that resemble the real object and then move on to pretending with imaginary objects.

Learning to substitute imaginary objects for real objects gives children flexibility in their pretend play. If a child always had to have a real object to play, the play themes would be less imaginative and creative. Sometimes when children are using substitute or imaginary objects you may not be able to tell what they are pretending. Watch their gestures and what they say to help you understand. Children use real-looking objects, substitute objects, and imaginary objects all together while playing. Children who cannot pretend with imaginary objects, especially by age four or five, will be tied to pretending with real objects and lack the flexibility to play with their peers.

One morning Anita walked around the learning environment with a unit block in her hand. She was putting it close to her mouth and mumbling something. Missy, the teacher, watched her and couldn't tell what she was doing. She walked over to Anita to tell her to return the block to the block area. Then she heard her state, "Over and out." She realized she was using it as a walkie-talkie. Missy encouraged her to go to the block area where the other children were playing riding the bus. Soon several of the children were using blocks as walkie-talkies.

Time to Reflect

How did Missy know what Anita was pretending? What opportunity would Anita have lost if Missy had just told her to put the block back?

_____

_____

_____

_____

I also had a little blue car that someone gave me and I had it for a long, long time. It was like the ones the farmers in the movies had. I would make little roads with it and dig in the dirt with it. You can play with earth and mud year-round. I just found it in my house and it's still there, buried and beat up, but it's there. Since it's plastic it lasts for fifty years. —Edgar, from Guatemala

Time to Reflect

Think about an older child in your learning environment. Describe how that child pretends with objects. What does the child like to use to pretend?

_____

_____

_____

_____

What to Look For

- What objects children use in play
- What they do with them
- What they say as they use them

Pretending with Objects Items

The following are the items in the Pretending with Objects section:
- Does not use objects to pretend: the child only manipulates objects or explores their properties.
- Uses real objects: the child pretends but only with objects that look real, such as a frying pan.
- Substitutes objects for other objects: the child pretends with objects that resemble the real object but aren't exactly like it.
- Uses imaginary objects: the child pretends with gestures and words, such as handing over imaginary money or imaginary food.

Look at the notes from your observation and the Pretending with Objects items described above. Check the level you consistently saw the child reach as you observed:

_____ Does not use objects to pretend

_____ Uses real objects

_____ Substitutes objects for other objects

_____ Uses imaginary objects

How did you choose the level you checked? What did you see the child doing during play?

_____

_____

_____

Remembering Families

Encourage families to pretend with their children. Ask family members to play along when children bring them imaginary money or food. Describe how their child pretends in the classroom and how pretending reflects the child's abilities. Advocate for toys that use imagination.

2 ROLE-PLAYING

Just as actors do in the theater, children take on roles as they play. While playing in the house area they may be the mom, the dad, the dog, or the child. While playing doctor, children pretend to be doctors, receptionists, nurses, and patients. To make their roles more realistic, they often dress up, pretend with the props, and use language that fits the role they are enacting.

Having roles that fit together into an entire play scenario enriches the play. Babies do not take on roles when they are little, but they do start to understand parts of roles early on. When you see a toddler pat a baby or pick up a telephone, they are starting to play a role. Eventually they put sequences together building toward acting out the whole role, including dress, voice, gestures, and language. If a child cannot take on a role in play in preschool, that child will be unable to join in a play scenario with other children.

☀ Chakra had just put a new dramatic play theme in by the house area. It was a pizza shop. She had included pizza boxes, pizza cutters, aprons, menus, and ordering pads. One child, Geraldo, watched the other children playing but he didn't enter the play. One morning he suddenly exclaimed, "I'm the pizza delivery guy!" Then he ran off. Chakra realized he didn't know exactly what to do as a pizza delivery person. She gave him a hat, helped him pick up the pizzas, and together they pretended to drive to houses (other learning areas) in the classroom. Once they were there, she asked him to give the pizza to children playing in that area and pretend to take their money. Geraldo played the delivery guy for several days.

Time to Reflect

What do you think Geraldo initially understood about being a pizza delivery person? Do you agree with Chakra's actions as a teacher? Why or why not?

_____

_____

_____

_____

What are the roles children play in the house area? How do you know who they are pretending to be?

_____

_____

_____

_____

What to Look For

- How children are dressed

- What props they are using

- What the theme is

- What tones and mannerisms they use when speaking

- What they are saying

Role-Playing Items

The following are the items in the Role-Playing section:

- No role play: the child does not use voice, dress, or gestures to indicate a role.

- Uses one sequence of play: the child will pretend to do one action or gesture to indicate a role, such as lifting a phone and putting it down.

- Combines sequences: the child puts sequences together to form a role, such as a mother who cooks, feeds a baby, and opens the refrigerator door.

- Uses verbal declaration: the child declares a role, such as a firefighter, but doesn't do any of the dress, voice, or actions to go with the declaration.

- Imitates actions of role, including dress: the child plays out, much like an actor, his perceptions of the role. A child pretending to be in the role of a police officer will pretend to drive a car, pursue bad guys, and have a police hat on.

Look at the notes from your observation and the Role-Playing items described above. Check the level you consistently saw the child reach as you observed:

_____ No role play

_____ Uses one sequence of play

_____ Combines sequences

_____ Uses verbal declaration (for example, "I'm a doctor")

_____ Imitates actions of role, including dress

How did you choose the level you checked? What role was your child playing and how did you know?

_____

_____

_____

I loved wandering the woods at our cabin in northern Minnesota. I would pretend I was an orphan, a runaway, a shipwrecked stowaway. The trees, lake, rocks, and pine needles all played their part in my story. I also loved pretending I was the heroine in a movie trailer (the most dramatic moments, really). —Carrie

Remembering Families

Children learn to play roles from watching the adults around them. Adults can help children understand how people act when they are doctors, firefighters, or teachers. For example, after going to the doctor, parents can talk about the instruments the doctor used such as the stethoscope or a syringe. They can point out how the doctor was dressed. They can ask the children what they noticed. When children have more understanding of adult roles, they will play the roles with greater depth.

3 VERBALIZATIONS ABOUT THE PLAY SCENARIO

Older children create stories as they play. Often they start their story with one child saying, "Let's pretend." Then other children add details. It is a collective story that helps children develop roles and determines how the story will play out.

Young children will start by using words to describe in simple terms how they are using an object. They may hand you a piece of paper and declare, "This is money." They move from describing an object or action to creating a whole story. If children cannot make this transition, they will not be able to keep up with the play around them. They may be left out or excluded.

Amad yelled at the other children in the dramatic play area, "It's a fire! It's a fire!" Children stopped and looked at Amad. He continued, "Let's pretend there is a fire and the firefighters come in their trucks and pour water on it." Amad put on the firefighter hat. One child started to tell children to leave the house area because there was a fire. Several children pretended to drive trucks to the house area. Amad went to the teacher and asked her for a hose. She brought out several cardboard tubes they could use as hoses. The children pretended to pour water on the fire.

Time to Reflect

How did Amad start the story about a fire in the dramatic play area? What might have happened if no other children had picked up the story? How did they pick up the story?

_____

_____

_____

_____

What to Look For

- What children are saying to their peers while playing

- What play theme is being developed

- What children say they are pretending

When children use language to pretend, they are giving you a window into their minds. Think back to a time you were a child. What were the scenarios you described with your friends as you played? Were they war stories? Or stories about babies and mothers? Or stories about teachers and school?

_____

_____

_____

_____

I loved my backyard. There was a fence around the lawn that had headers every six feet. My friends and I would tie ropes around them and straddle the fence to pretend we were riding horses. We would pretend we were riding the range. We all watched Channel 7 *Roundup* on Saturdays and would reenact the plots all the next week. —JoAnn

Usually with a sibling or neighbor we would agree to carry out a plan together. —Rita

I also remember playing pretend based on stories in books or movies. Once my brother, friend, and I pretended we were living in Nazi Germany. We made a shack out of blankets under Reid's bunk bed and we wore costumes. The actual play involved sneaking to the market to buy things we needed. We even turned off the lights and used flashlights so it was sneakier. —Marcia

Verbalizations about the Play Scenario Items

The following are the items in the Verbalizations about the Play Scenario section:
- Does not use pretend words during play: the child may not be using words during pretend sequences; the child may or may not have language delays.
- Uses words to describe substitute objects: the child will help you understand what the object represents by using words (for example, the child gives you a block and says, "This is a piece of pie.")
- Uses words to describe imaginary objects and actions (for example, "I'm painting a house"): the child will gesture and explain actions through words.
- Uses words to create a play scenario (for example, "Let's say we're being taken by a monster"): the child will create a narrative or story to bring the whole group together to play out the story.

Look at the notes from your observation and the Verbalizations about Play Scenario items described above. Check the level you consistently saw the child reach as you observed:

_____ Does not use pretend words during play

_____ Uses words to describe substitute objects

_____ Uses words to describe imaginary objects and actions (for example, "I'm painting a house")

_____ Uses words to create a play scenario (for example, "Let's say we're being taken by a monster")

How did you choose the level you checked? What did you see the child doing during play?

_____

_____

_____

Time to Reflect

What creative scenarios have children initiated in your learning environment? What kinds of props do they ask for? What sparked the scenario? Was it a certain prop, or a book, or a television show?

_____

_____

_____

_____

When children form play scenarios together, they are telling a story. Encourage families to read and tell stories with their children. Ask them to talk with their children about the story. Let children fill in details and, sometimes, determine the direction of the story.

4 VERBAL COMMUNICATION DURING A PLAY EPISODE

In order to develop a play theme or scenario, children need to communicate with each other. They may say they don't like how another player is acting out a role. They may say they want props that are more realistic. They may say they want the story line to go a certain way.

As in the other sections, children don't start with communicating with other children. They begin by talking to themselves as they play. You may have noticed a toddler talking away about what he is doing as he pretends to cook or set the table. Children will often tell adults how they want the play to go. As they get older they communicate directly with the other children in the group. The most sophisticated players can communicate through a role to bring other players together. If a child cannot do this, story lines will be impossible to develop as a group.

What to Look For

- What children are saying to one another
- What tones and mannerisms they use when speaking
- What other children do with the communication

☀ Jaime and a small group of boys were playing fishing. They had a pretend boat and fishing poles. Jaime loudly proclaimed, "I see a shark over there." All of the children looked where he was pointing. One child said, "I don't see it." Jaime said, "It's underwater and it is coming toward us. We have to get away from here. Let's start rowing." The children screamed a little bit and laughed as they pretended to row to land. The fishing poles were forgotten in the water.

Time to Reflect

How did Jaime help the other children know what he wanted in this example?

_____

_____

_____

_____

When children play, they sometimes tell others what they should do in their roles. Can you remember a time when children told you what you had to say or do in a role? What kinds of things did they tell you to do? What was the theme?

_____

_____

What happens when one child tells other children how they should act in their roles?

_____

_____

_____

_____

Verbal Communication during a Play Episode Items

The following are the items in the Verbal Communication during a Play Episode section:

- Does not verbally communicate during play: the child does not use words to communicate with peers while playing together.
- Talks during play only to self: the child doesn't communicate with others but will talk to self while playing.
- Talks only to adults in play: the child doesn't communicate with peers but will talk with adults while playing.
- Talks with peers in play by stepping outside of role (for example, "That's not how mothers hold their babies"): the child communicates with children about their roles by coming out of role to do so.
- Talks with peers from within role (for example, "Eat your dinner before your dad comes home"): the child communicates through role to peers about what he wants.

Look at the notes from your observation and the Verbal Communication during a Play Episode items described above. Check the level you consistently saw the child reach as you observed:

____ Does not verbally communicate during play

____ Talks during play only to self

____ Talks only to adults in play

_____ Talks with peers in play by stepping outside of role (for example, "That's not how mothers hold their babies")

_____ Talks with peers from within role (for example, "Eat your dinner before your dad comes home")

How did you choose the level you checked? What did you see the child doing during play?

_____

_____

_____

Time to Reflect

Sometimes children can be quite bossy when they are communicating about roles and have a need to control the play. How do you feel about this behavior? How do the other children react?

_____

_____

_____

_____

Remembering Families

Conversation in families can be rich and complex. Point out to families that children learn language by hearing a large vocabulary and expressing themselves in their homes. If children have a home language other than English, ask families to use their home language whenever possible to help the children develop a solid vocabulary in that language. Send home conversation starters based on themes you are studying. Include dramatic play themes you have introduced.

5   PERSISTENCE IN PLAY

Children spend much of their playtime setting up for the play scenario. They have to decide on the story line, choose or get the props, and decide the roles. After they set up, we want them to play the scenario with the group for at least ten minutes. Anything shorter than that and they will not realize the benefits of sociodramatic play, which is a group of children playing together with pretend roles. Active children and children with short attention spans often struggle with this area.

✳ Kelley entered the house area to play. A couple of girls joined her and started to set up the house and put the babies to bed. Kelley pretended she was the mom for about three minutes. She held the baby, rocked it, and put it in the crib. Then she left the area even though the other girls tried to call her back to play with them.

Time to Reflect

Kelley left the play after only a few minutes. Why do you think she might have left the play?

_____

_____

_____

_____

If a child in your care consistently plays with children for such a short time, what do you do?

_____

_____

_____

Think of a child in your care with a short attention span. What happens when she is playing with a group of children? What happens to the play with other children when she leaves?

_____

_____

_____

What to Look For

Keep track of how much time the child plays after setting up. You can use a timer or stopwatch to measure how much time a child is spending in actual play.

Persistence in Play Items

The following are the items in the Persistence in Play section:
- Less than five minutes: the child can only stay in group play less than five minutes. This is common for children three years old or younger.
- Six to nine minutes: the child stays six to nine minutes. This is common for four-year-olds.
- Ten minutes or longer: the child can sustain a sociodramatic play episode for over ten minutes. This is expected for five-year-olds.

Look at the notes from your observation and the Persistence in Play items described above. Check the level you consistently saw the child reach as you observed:

_____ Less than five minutes

_____ Six to nine minutes

_____ Ten minutes or longer

How did you choose the level you checked? What did you see the child doing during play?

_____

_____

_____

Time to Reflect

Think about children who are active and always moving. What do you do to help a child stop and focus?

_____

_____

_____

_____

Finding ways to help a child stop and focus can be tiring for a teacher. How do you take care of yourself when you have challenging children in your group?

_____

_____

_____

_____

Remembering Families

Families can help children stay with a task longer if they eliminate distractions and do the task with the children. If they have asked children to clean up their rooms, divide the task into smaller units, such as "First we put away the shirts, and then we will pick up the shoes from the floor." They can offer to help. If their attention starts to flag, they can take a break and come back to the task.

Help parents understand how important it is for children to learn to persist, even if the task is hard. Children who come back again and again to master a task demonstrate more success in school.

6   INTERACTIONS

One of the motivating factors for preschool children is the opportunity to play with others. Babies' first play partners are the important adults in their lives—parents, grandparents, and caregivers. As they grow and develop, they learn to play alone. As they get older, children's interactions include play with one other child and then play with a group of children.

This development doesn't progress in a rigid fashion but in a general way. Children who don't play with others and instead only play alone may miss the lessons group play can give them. When children play with others, they learn how to solve conflict, how to plan a play scenario together, how to listen to others, and how to stand up for themselves.

☀ Olivia was sitting alone in the corner. When Lyle, the teacher, asked her what was going on and why she wasn't playing with others, Olivia just shrugged her shoulders. When Lyle asked her again, she said her friend wasn't there. She stated, "I can only play with her." Lyle pointed out another group of children were playing in the dramatic play area. There was a doctor corner set up. Lyle told her that they needed someone to run the X-ray machine. Olivia shook her head no, but then got up when Lyle took her hand. Lyle took her to the doctor's office and said, "Here's Olivia. She knows how to do the X-ray machine." The children lined up to get their X-rays taken. Olivia had a serious expression on her face but kept playing with the X-ray machine until it was time to clean up.

Time to Reflect

How do you think Olivia felt about playing without her friend?

_____

_____

_____

_____

Do you agree with how Lyle handled Olivia's refusal to play? Why or why not?

_____

_____

_____

_____

How do you think Olivia felt about it?

_____

_____

_____

This is somewhat painful for me because I felt awkward in making friends—had a few single friends over the years that I became close to. —Becky

We always lived in pretty remote areas so there weren't many kids around until I was in third grade. I didn't always have a best friend until eighth grade. —Kara

My cousins were the same age. We had a blast. I did not know until I went to elementary school that people played with people that were not their cousins. It was a new concept. —Claire

I have the most fun with my friends when we laugh and giggle together. —Alivia, age 6

Time to Reflect

When you remember how you played when you were young, do you remember if you played more alone or with others?

_____

_____

What do you remember playing?

_____

_____

_____

_____

What to Look For

- Whom the child usually plays with

- When the child plays alone and when the child plays with others

- What the child does when playing with others or alone

Interactions Items

The following are the items in the Interactions section:

- Plays alone: the child plays by self, often with materials, such as Lego blocks, that encourage solitary play.
- Plays only with adults: the child prefers to play with adults and avoids play experiences with peers.
- Plays with one child, always the same person: the child always wants to play with a special friend and is distraught when the friend isn't there.
- Plays with one child, can be different partners: the child can play with one other child, but when groups gets larger, leaves group or begins to fight over toys.
- Can play with two or three children together: the child is able to play with a group and pay attention to the roles, story, and other children's participation.

Look at the notes from your observation and the Interactions items described above. Check the level you consistently saw the child reach as you observed:

_____ Plays alone
_____ Plays only with adults
_____ Plays with one child, always the same person
_____ Plays with one child, can be different partners
_____ Can play with two or three children together

How did you choose the level you checked? What did you see the child doing during play?

_____

_____

_____

Remembering Families

If children don't have a natural play group such as a neighborhood group, siblings, or cousins, suggest that families arrange playtimes with friends. Children can't learn to be successful in their interactions with other children unless they have practice.

7 ENTRANCE INTO A PLAY GROUP

Entering an ongoing play group can be a difficult balancing act. Sometimes children can enter too forcefully and be rejected or stand outside of the group and be rejected. The child who learns how to stand close to the group in play or get the attention of at least one child in the group will be more successful than the child who just asks, "Can I play?" Yet this is the strategy we often suggest children try when they want to play with others.

If children cannot learn the successful strategies, they may become discouraged about trying. They may feel bad about themselves or angry at their peers. Either way they are missing out on the learning group play can provide.

☀ Tawnya watched the children playing in the house area every day. But she didn't try to enter the play or talk with the children playing with dolls and cooking at the stove. She stayed outside of the play and looked very serious. She seemed to inch closer and closer to the play. When her teachers suggested she go into the house area to play, she just stood there. But when one of the teachers brought her a doll and asked her to take care of the baby, Tawnya brought the doll into the house area and started to sing to it.

Time to Reflect

How did the teacher help Tawnya enter the group?

_____

_____

_____

_____

What would you have done?

_____

_____

_____

_____

I distinctly remember one time I was playing house with a friend from down the block. My little brother kept barging in, and when I complained to my mom she said we had to include him. Our solution was to make my poor little two-year-old brother be the postman just long enough to deliver his letters and then he had to leave the room. —Carrie

Although we may feel like children are being mean when they exclude another child, sometimes the reasons for the rejection are more complicated. Sometimes children can't figure out how to include another child. For example, if the group already has a dad, they may not understand how they could include another dad.

You can help the group by making suggestions. Talk about how the group could add more babies so there could be two dads. Helping the group problem solve their dilemmas will lead to more success for all of the children.

Time to Reflect

Think back to a time when you went to a party where you didn't know many people. What kind of strategies did you use to enter into groups already in conversation? What kind of insight does this give you about how children might try to enter a group?

_____

_____

_____

_____

What to Look For
- What children do when they want to play with a group of children
- What children say when they want to play with a group of children
- How other children respond to them

Entrance into a Play Group Items

The following are the items in the Entrance into a Play Group section:
- Does not attempt to enter play group: the child will not attempt to enter group. The child often will play alone.
- Uses force to enter play group: the child may poke, hit, threaten, or destroy other children's work to gain entrance to the play group.
- Stands near group and watches: the child stands close to group and sometimes gets integrated into play.
- Imitates behavior of group: the child plays near group doing similar activities on the outskirts of the group. The group sometimes surrounds her and she is part of the play.
- Makes comments related to play theme: the child comes into group and makes a comment related to play. For example, if the group is playing babies, the child may say, "The baby is crying."
- Gets attention of another child before commenting: the child uses an effective way to get into group by saying a child's name who is already playing, then making the comment.

Look at the notes from your observation and the Entrance into a Play Group items described above. Check the level you consistently saw the child reach as you observed:
____ Does not attempt to enter play group
____ Uses force to enter play group
____ Stands near group and watches
____ Imitates behavior of group
____ Makes comments related to play theme
____ Gets attention of another child before commenting

How did you choose the level you checked? What did you see the child doing during play?

_____

_____

_____

Time to Reflect

Watching a child being excluded can be heartbreaking. Although you may want to rush in and force the other children to include him, it is sometimes more helpful to teach the child successful strategies to use. What is your response when a child is being excluded in your learning environment? What have you tried? How have children responded?

_____

_____

_____

_____

Remembering Families

If a child is feeling excluded or avoids playing in groups, parents may feel concerned. Share your observations and some of your strategies with them. Suggest they invite just one child over to play at first. When their child is comfortable playing with one other child, try a small group of children. When children have friends in the group, they are more likely to be successful in their attempts to enter ongoing play. Reassure parents that it takes practice to learn to make friends and play in a group.

8   PROBLEM SOLVING

Children have many problems during play. They want a toy another child has; they may not be able to find the toys they want; they may not want to play what the other children want to play. How a child approaches these challenges will determine how well and how often they are solved to the child's benefit. Some children may try to solve problems or conflicts with force. Sometimes the force may be only threatened, but other children cooperate out of fear. Other children may always give in to other children and not express their thoughts and feelings.

In this section we give strategies to help children learn to propose and accept compromises. It takes a great deal of time and practice for children to learn how to do this. If a child cannot problem solve, strategies of using force or just giving up will increasingly mean the child will be left out of the group. Your support and guidance are key to helping a child learn to solve her own problems. Sometimes we encourage children just to solve things on their own. We need to give them the tools before they are able to solve problems independently.

☀ Annie and Patrick were playing taking the train. They had set up chairs in a row and were writing out tickets in the writing center. They invited other children to come and ride the train. Annie started taking tickets and Patrick pushed her away and took the tickets away from her. She went and sat in the engineer's seat and pretended to toot the horn. Patrick ran over and said, "I'm the engineer. I drive the train." Annie just looked at him, frowned, and got up from the seat. She left the area to play somewhere else.

Time to Reflect

What did you see in this example? What did Patrick want and how did he get it? How did Annie react? If you saw this happening in your learning environment, what would you do?

_____

_____

_____

_____

Most of the conflicts I had with friends were with my girlfriends, over dolls or playing house, because I didn't like playing with dolls or playing dress up. Most of the time it was solved by me giving in and playing what they wanted to play for a while. They were not tomboys so they did not want to play sport-type games. —Kim

I am sad when my friends hurt my feelings and we don't get along. I solve it by saying, "Can you please stop?" And saying sorry. —Alivia, age 6

What to Look For

- What kinds of conflicts children have

- What they do when they have a conflict or problem

- What kind of support they seek out

- What conflicts are about

Problem-Solving Items

The following are the items in the Problem-Solving section:
- Gives in during conflict: the child gives up toy, leaves area, or goes to another activity when challenged.
- Uses force to solve problems: the child uses verbal threats or physical intimidation to get what he wants.
- Seeks adult assistance: the child will come to an adult for help. The child may cry, complain, or just seek out the adult.

- Imitates verbal solutions or strategies provided by adults: the child will use the words adult gives him when adult provides them.
- Recalls words or strategies to use when reminded: the child will use the words adult has given him when reminded.
- Initiates use of words or strategies: the child will use words on own without assistance of adult.
- Accepts reasonable compromises: the child can use own words to propose and accept compromises with other children.

Look at your notes from your observation and the Problem-Solving items described above. Check the level you consistently saw the child reach as you observed:

_____ Gives in during conflict

_____ Uses force to solve problems

_____ Seeks adult assistance

_____ Imitates verbal solutions or strategies provided by adults

_____ Recalls words or strategies to use when reminded

_____ Initiates use of words or strategies

_____ Accepts reasonable compromises

How did you choose the level you checked? What did you see the child doing during play?

_____

_____

_____

Using Problem-Solving Steps

When you see the item "Seeks adult assistance," you may be reminded of children who often seek your help when they are upset. They may tattle, whine, or constantly interrupt you to complain about their peers' behavior. Look at this item as part of a continuum. The children who solve problems by force, or who always give up when facing a problem, need the support and assistance of an adult to move beyond the methods they are using. You don't want the children to stay at that level. You want them to start imitating the words you give them. For example, if you were working with Annie in our beginning example, you would ask her to come to you for help when Patrick pushed her out of the way. Then you could give her the words to use. "Annie, tell Patrick you want to take tickets." Eventually she will learn to express her feelings without your help.

Teach children the steps of problem solving:

1. Identify the problem

2. Gather information

3. Brainstorm solutions

4. Pick the best idea

5. Try it

6. Decide if it is working

7. Revise if needed

> I don't remember asking adults for help except when Ted got stuck on the rope swing overhanging the river! This affirmed my own fear of the rope swing: you had to do it just right and let go at the right time or you would get stuck hanging over the river. The Navesink River came from the ocean and was brackish, which allowed jellyfish to thrive in the shallow water. I remember the fathers all came running with ladders. (I am sure their worry was the water itself and the shallowness of the river, but for me it was those jellyfish.) —Beth

Remembering Families

It is very easy (and sometimes necessary) for adults to jump in when children are having problems with each other. Families are often distressed when children are fighting and either want to stop it or solve it quickly. Share with families the ways you are teaching children to solve their problems with each other. Encourage them to try the same techniques at home.

9   TURN TAKING

Taking turns is hard for children to learn. The process of taking turns begins very early, as babies coo back and forth with their parents or loved ones. But sharing a beloved toy becomes a challenge for young children. They often grab the toy away from other children or refuse to give it up. Sometimes they leave it but still think it is theirs and protest when some other child picks it up.

As children grow older they learn that sharing can benefit them as well as the other child. They learn that when they share, others will share with them. When they share, other children will more likely stay and play longer. Learning to take turns requires much assistance from adults at first. If children cannot take turns, other children will start to turn away from them and avoid playing with them.

☀ Terrance ran to pick up the ball in the play yard. He held it tightly to his chest. Mai, the teacher, encouraged him to throw it to Lin. Terrance shook his head no. Mai walked over to him and explained that he and Lin would have fun throwing it back and forth. Terrance wouldn't let go of the ball. Eventually Lin ran over to the slide and climbed up the ladder. Other children followed her. Terrance sat down by the tree and rolled the ball around.

Time to Reflect

If you had Terrance in your learning environment, what would you do?

_____

_____

_____

_____

Some toys are clearly harder for children to share than others. What toys and props are difficult to share?

What toys are easier to share?

_____

_____

_____

_____

What to Look For

- When the child is willing to take turns

- What the child does when asked to take turns

- What the child does when another child refuses to take turns

- What helps the child take turns

Turn Taking Items

The following are the items in the Turn Taking section:
- Refuses to take turns: the child (often a toddler or young preschooler) will refuse to take turns even if directed by an adult.
- Leaves toys, then protests when others pick them up: the child will put down a toy, but when another takes it, will cry and protest as if she had it still.
- Takes turns if arranged and directed by an adult: the child needs an adult to structure the turn taking. If this support is given, the child will agree to give up toys.
- Asks for turn, does not wait for a response: the child can use words, but takes the toy before other child answers. The child doesn't wait for an answer.
- Gives up toy easily if done with it: an older child will share more easily if the child is finished with the toy.

- Gives up toy if another child asks for it: the child is still playing with the toy but will give to the other child if asked.
- Proposes turn taking, will take and give turns: the child gives up toy, asks for toy, and will offer a toy to help keep play going.

Look at the notes from your observation and the Turn Taking items described above. Check the level you consistently saw the child reach as you observed:

_____ Refuses to take turns

_____ Leaves toys, then protests when others pick them up

_____ Takes turns if arranged and directed by an adult

_____ Asks for turn, does not wait for a response

_____ Gives up toy easily if done with it

_____ Gives up toy if another child asks for it

_____ Proposes turn taking, will take and give turns

How did you choose the level you checked? What did you see the child doing during play?

_____

_____

_____

Time to Reflect

One helpful strategy for teaching children to problem solve is by watching puppets as they work out a conflict. Write a play for two puppets about turn taking. Here's the scene: two puppets are building a tower and one puppet won't share any of the blocks. What happens next? Include how the puppets learn to take turns.

_____

_____

_____

_____

Act out the play with the children in your group. What was their response?

_____

_____

_____

_____

Taking turns is part of being a family. Encourage families to talk about taking turns as they do so. Ask them to comment on how well children are taking turns. Play games where children have to take turns to play, such as rolling or throwing a ball back and forth.

10   SUPPORT OF PEERS

This section is about helping children show empathy toward others, especially their peers. Babies have a contagious empathy that is apparent when one baby starts crying in a group of babies. Soon all of them start crying. As children get older, they may show that support and empathy or they may not. If they are also very upset, they may not notice another child's distress. But when they are able to notice that another child is upset, they may offer help or comfort. Eventually, older preschoolers can share ideas with others and encourage their peers. If children cannot do this, their peers will not seek them out. The most popular children are those who are able to give support to others.

☀ Chue was happily playing with the Lego blocks. Several other boys joined him at the table. One boy became upset when a block fell off his building. When the block fell, his whole building started to fall apart. Chue looked up and watched his friend. Then he looked at the building. He took a few of the blocks and said he would help him build it again. His friend stopped crying and handed Chue some more Lego blocks.

Time to Reflect

What did you see Chue doing? How was he showing empathy?

_____

_____

_____

_____

What to Look For

• What children do when their peers are upset

• How they offer help

• What kind of help they offer

• How they offer and take suggestions of peers

I remember feeling the need to treat all of my stuffed animals equally. I tried to play with them all the same amount, always sleep with all of them. I didn't think it was fair to have a favorite stuffed animal. —Amanda

Time to Reflect

Describe a time when you felt empathy for a child in your setting. How did you show your empathy? How did the child respond?

_____

_____

_____

_____

Support of Peers Items

The following are the items in the Support of Peers section:

- Shows no interest in peers: the child ignores peers and does not notice feelings of other children. The child may be distracted, distressed, or have a special need that affects her ability to notice the feelings of others.
- Directs attention to distress of peers: the child notices when other children are upset. May move closer to the other children or look at them intently.
- Shows empathy or offers help: the child notices distress of other children and offers to help.
- Offers and takes suggestions of peers at times: the child can share ideas and take ideas of other children during play.
- Encourages or praises peers: the child comments on strengths of other children.

Look at the notes from your observation and the Support of Peers items described above. Check the level you consistently saw the child reach as you observed:

_____ Shows no interest in peers

_____ Directs attention to distress of peers

_____ Shows empathy or offers help

_____ Offers and takes suggestions of peers at times

_____ Encourages or praises peers

How did you choose the level you checked? What did you see the child doing during play?

_____

_____

_____

Time to Reflect

Feeling empathy and offering help are very difficult for preschool children because they are often egocentric or self-absorbed. But sometimes we don't notice when children do show empathy. Think back on the past few days in your learning environment. How have you seen children showing empathy? How did you let them know you noticed it?

_____

_____

_____

_____

Remembering Families

Encourage families to read books about helping others and point out when adults and children are helping others. Have them talk as families about ways they have helped others and how it makes everyone feel. Perhaps most importantly, children learn empathy from how they are treated. Remind families to listen to their children's feelings and respond compassionately.

Justine, age 9

The Play Checklist was designed to help you plan ways to support children in their play skills. Although you filled out the checklist for one child, you could also fill it out for all the children in your group or fill out one section for several children struggling with similar issues. The next chapter assists you in writing a goal and creating a plan to help the child you observed.

Time to Reflect

What was your experience of filling out the checklist? What were your questions as you filled it out?

_____

_____

_____

_____

What puzzled you about the child's play skills while completing the checklist?

_____

_____

_____

CHAPTER 6 Planning Your Focus and Strategies

Once you have completed the Play Checklist, you will be able to see more clearly where the child is struggling during play. With this information you will be able to write a goal and plan activities. Sometimes a child will be struggling in just one of the checklist sections, such as Verbalizations about the Play Scenario or Problem Solving, but often children experience challenges in several of the checklist sections because they are all interrelated. When a child has several problem areas, planning a focus can be difficult. What should be the priority? It is tempting to work on all the challenges together. It is most effective, however, if you choose one area to focus on. By choosing a focus, you can more easily judge how well your strategies work.

Sometimes you may have several children struggling in the same area, for example, Problem Solving or Interactions. Our companion book, *When Play Isn't Fun*, offers suggestions to help children play more successfully in groups.

Content in this chapter connects with chapters 6 and 8 in *Play: The Pathway from Theory to Practice.*

Time to Reflect

Now that you have completed all ten items of the Play Checklist, look back over the sections. List the most challenging section or sections for the child you observed.

_____

_____

_____

_____

Look at your list of challenging areas. Choose one:

_____

Why did you choose this area for the child?

_____

_____

_____

_____

The items in each section are designed to go from the easiest to the most advanced play skill. Look closely at the section you highlighted. Now highlight the item within the section you checked. It should be the level you consistently saw the child reach as you observed.

_____

Now write down the next item in the section.

_____

Setting Goals

The item you wrote down in the preceding reflection will be your goal for the child. Writing a goal can be much harder than it sounds. But the items on the checklist give you a step-by-step guide. The following anecdote provides an example of writing a goal from the checklist.

☀ Patricia had just filled out the Play Checklist on Sidney. Sidney had challenges in several sections: Role-Playing, Persistence in Play, and Problem Solving. After thinking about how much Sidney wanted to play with others and how difficult it was for him to do that, Patricia decided to focus on Role-Playing. If Sidney started to have some success playing a role with others, maybe the fighting would lessen and he would play longer. Patricia had checked "Uses verbal declaration." The next item down is "Imitates actions of role, including dress." Patricia wrote the following goal based on that next item:

Who: Sidney
Does what: imitates the actions of a role with his peers
Where: in the dramatic play area
How well or how often: two out of four days a week
By when: by winter term
Patricia's goal for Sidney: Sidney will imitate the actions of a role with his peers in the dramatic play area two out of four days a week by winter term.

This format will work when you write any goal. Fill out the following form to write down a goal for the child you are working with.

Goal Setting

Who: _____

Does what: _____

Where: _____

How well or how often: _____

By when: _____

Your goal: _____

_____

Now the Strategies

Once you have determined your focus and written your goal for the child, it is time to choose activities and strategies. Maybe you have already thought of strategies that will work in your learning environment, but here is a chart to further assist you. The chart lists each section of the Play Checklist with some possible strategies. In addition, effective language techniques for English-language learners and children with language delays are highlighted in the last part of the chapter. There are many more strategies in our book *Play*, and you can make up some of your own.

STRATEGIES DURING PLAY

Play Checklist Sections	Activities and Strategies to Try during Play
Pretending with Objects	• Have many real or real-looking objects for the child to use when pretending. • Gradually include objects that could substitute for many things, such as blocks for food. • Model using imaginary objects, such as money or food. These are usually the first imaginary objects children use.
Role-Playing	• Provide dress-up clothes the child may recognize, such as for a doctor or firefighter. • Suggest roles with less language that the child can play, such as a family pet or the baby of the family. • Model a role for the child, such as a doctor. Have lab coats, X-rays, and doctor equipment available. • Encourage the child to play a role such as doctor to a doll rather than to another child at first.
Verbalizations about the Play Scenario	• Encourage the child to describe substitute or imaginary objects if he hands them to you. • If the child isn't speaking in your learning environment, use language techniques such as self-talk, parallel talk, and expansion. (See section after the charts for more explanation.) • Play with the child or a group and start by creating a scenario such as, "Let's say Lily is feeling sick and . . ." Then ask the child to add a few details. Play out the scenario as the child created it.
Verbal Communication during a Play Episode	• If the child isn't speaking in your learning environment, use language techniques such as self-talk, parallel talk, and expansion. • Sit near the child while he is playing and coach him about words to use with other children as they play. Ask him to tell his friend to pour the coffee, for example. • Model verbally communicating while playing a role. Direct your comments to children who aren't speaking as much as others. • Pair the child with a verbal child to play together in an area.
Persistence in Play	• To lengthen the child's attention span, play next to the child. • Combine dramatic play with sensorimotor material such as water or sand. Children will tend to play longer. • Set up a dramatic play theme that will attract the child and hold her attention. • Set up a dramatic play theme outside, such as a car wash or washing clothes. • Bring in new props when the child loses interest in play.
Interactions	• Use the Play Checklist to decide whether to have the child play with you, with another child, or with a group of children. • Set up a play experience that doesn't require as much interaction, such as puzzles, playdough, or blocks with attractive props. • Combine a dramatic play theme with sensorimotor materials, such as washing babies. This attracts children but doesn't require as much interaction at first. • Play with children to encourage interactions between them.

STRATEGIES DURING PLAY

Play Checklist Sections	Activities and Strategies to Try during Play
Entrance into a Play Group	• Coach the child to stand near a group of children who are playing. • Play with the child, imitating the actions of the group. • Model making comments related to the play before joining a group. • Coach the child to make comments related to play of a group before attempting to join the group. • Encourage the child to get attention of one child before making comment. • Help the child learn new ways to join a group if she has tried to enter by being destructive. Point out that children won't want to play with her when she pushes them or knocks down their buildings.
Problem Solving	• Encourage the child to seek your help when first learning to solve problems. • When there is a conflict, ask the child to help you think of solutions. • Encourage the child to listen to others' ideas. • Encourage the child to try solutions, then talk with you about how it went.
Turn Taking	• Structure turns with popular toys with a timer or a waiting list. • If you see children grabbing toys, intervene and ask them to ask the child for a turn. • Have enough toys to cut down on disagreements, especially over popular toys. • Model taking turns while in dramatic play.
Support of Peers	• When you are helping a child who is hurt or upset, talk about how you are helping the child. • Talk about your own feelings and how children are helping you. • Model taking care of babies during play. • Set up play themes that encourage taking care of others, such as a house, doctor's office, and a veterinary clinic.

Some Play Checklist items lend themselves to teaching strategies and discussions outside of play during large groups, small groups, large-motor time, and transitions. These lessons outside of play amplify the work you have done during play. The following chart provides suggestions for these lessons for each section of the Play Checklist.

STRATEGIES FOR OUTSIDE OF PLAY

Play Checklist Sections	Strategies Outside of Play
Pretending with Objects	• Act out pretend experiences during large group, such as driving the bus or going swimming. • Use transition times to pretend to skate to the next room or paint an imaginary wall. • During a small group, give each child a doll and have the children pretend to feed their babies and put the babies to sleep. • Act out imaginary actions, such as cleaning and cooking, and ask children to guess what you are doing.
Role-Playing	• Pretend to be a bird or another animal during transitions. • Act out simple nursery rhymes such as "Jack Be Nimble." • Act out simple stories such as "The Three Billy Goats Gruff." • Provide a flannel board for children to act out a story with flannel-board props.
Verbalizations about the Play Scenario	• Use a pretend microphone and ask individual children questions, such as "What is your favorite toy?" • Perform a puppet show where one puppet suggests a play theme and both puppets give ideas.
Verbal Communication during a Play Episode	• Ask the child to talk with puppets. • Create small-group murals and help each child to talk about their part. • Dismiss children from group by asking a question and recording their answer. • Play a game during large group where you start a movement and then everyone copies the movement; then ask other children to lead first.
Persistence in Play	• Encourage the child to listen during group by letting her hold small props or a pillow. • When the child starts to leave an activity, point out something new to add new interest. • Let the child be the leader in activities and point out his leadership.
Interactions	• Pair children to do activities, such as painting or running errands around the room. • Teach the child to respond each time another child speaks to him. • Give a small group of children a task such as creating a mural or building something. Then take a picture of their accomplishment.
Entrance into a Play Group	• Play copycat with objects. Give each child in a small group the same materials. Ask them to copy what you do, such as rock the doll or drive the truck. • Point out that children who play together often do the same activities. • Discuss with children how you enter a group. Give examples and ask what they would do. • Encourage children to call your name rather than tap you on the shoulder. • Make up a story or act out a puppet play where one puppet wants to play and pushes others to get into a group. Discuss with the children how to help the puppet.

Play Checklist Sections	Strategies Outside of Play
Problem Solving	• Encourage children to ask for help by pointing out how you ask for help. • Model how you solve problems by talking about how you solve situations, for example, not being able to reach materials. • Read books about how children solve problems. • Do a puppet play about solving problems.
Turn Taking	• Practice taking turns by rolling balls or cars back and forth. Point out how you are taking turns. • Play turn-taking board games and circle games. • Have children practice trading toys. • Have pairs of children make a picture together and decide how to share it.
Support of Peers	• Label other people's feelings as you notice them. • Show a picture of a child who is distressed. Ask children for suggestions for how to help the child. • Ask a small group of children to do a group picture. Each child adds a part of the picture. • Ask children to say something friendly when a peer does well.

Language Techniques: Self-Talk, Parallel Talk, and Expansion

During play, children use language to describe their play scenario, play roles, and communicate with fellow players. Children with language delays or English-language learners can be left behind in a fast-moving scenario. They can especially benefit from three language techniques: self-talk, parallel talk, and expansion. Use these in your learning environment to increase children's use of language.

• Self-talk: adult describes her actions. While setting the table for snack, she may say, "I'm putting down the plate first and then the napkin."

• Parallel talk: adult describes what the child is doing. For example, the adult may be playing in the sand table next to a child and say, "First Amy fills up her cup and then she pours it out."

• Expansion: adult expands on what the child says. The child may say, "More juice." The adult may expand by saying, "You want more juice in your cup."

As you use these techniques, remember that you are not correcting the child's language; you are simply providing a model for the child. These techniques are highly effective and help children both understand language and express themselves.

When you narrow your focus to one goal and plan activities and strategies around that goal, you will see more progress. You will be more able to measure and assess how the child is doing. Sometimes it can be frustrating to choose the focus because you may see several possible goals and you want to do it all. Your instruction will become more intentional and creative with this defining focus.

Time to Reflect

As you wrote a goal for the child you observed and chose strategies, what was the hardest thing to do?

_____

_____

_____

_____

What made it difficult?

_____

_____

_____

_____

What would have made it easier?

_____

_____

_____

_____

CHAPTER 7 **Planning Your Role**

Content in this chapter connects with chapter 7 in *Play: The Pathway from Theory to Practice*.

In several places in the preceding chapter, we referred to the adult role as a model, a coach, and a fellow player. Thinking about your role and deciding how you want to relate to the child while playing is a key part of the strategy. Sometimes you may join in the play; at other times you may make suggestions from the sidelines. The following chart describes the kinds of roles you could adopt during play.

ROLES FOR ADULTS

Adult Roles in Play	Description of Role	Benefits for Adult	Benefits for Child
Observer	• Adult sits near child and observes play • May occasionally make comments	• Gains valuable information	• Feels play is valued
Stage Manager	• Adult sets up play experience • Gives comments and suggestions if needed • Finds added props and play materials to support children's play	• Has opportunities to coach children during play • Learns children's interests when gathering props	• Gains support and resources • Feels play is valued
Parallel Player	• Adult plays near child with same materials, but does not address child directly	• Observes child's reactions • Builds relationship with child	• Lengthens attention span • Gains more confidence, especially a shy child

ROLES FOR ADULTS

Adult Roles in Play	Description of Role	Benefits for Adult	Benefits for Child
Co-player	• Adult joins ongoing play • Influences play by asking questions	• Extends play • Motivates children to join play • Introduces new ideas	• Retains control of play • Learns new play ideas • Feels play is valued and supported
Play Leader	• Adult begins play and takes more of a leadership role • Models new play behaviors • Models new dramatic theme	• Introduces new play behaviors • Introduces new dramatic play theme • Observes children's reactions	• Observes new play behaviors • Participates in new play behaviors • Learns about props and vocabulary for new dramatic play theme

Selecting a Role

To decide on your role, reflect on your goal, the child's needs, and what works well with your group. For example, if your goal is to help the child enter a play group, it may be most effective to be a stage manager providing suggestions to the child. If your goal is to help a child act out a role, it may be most effective to be a play leader at first, where you act out a role as a model. The play leader role is most intrusive to children's play and is to be used only for a short time. It is a powerful model for children, but it is important to let children move into control of their play as soon as possible. To decide which role to use, think about the following factors:

- how much difficulty the child is experiencing
- how new the theme is
- how much experience the child has with the theme, roles, and activities
- what play behaviors you want to model
- your goal
- your own comfort level

The following chart lists a play situation and an example of an adult role to use, plus an explanation why this role would work. Complete the last two examples.

ROLE OPTIONS

Situation	Adult Role to Use	Why?
Marnie was playing house with two other girls. She was frantically looking around for a pitcher to pour the pretend milk in a bowl. She ran to the teacher and asked her to get a pitcher.	Stage Manager: The teacher found a pitcher and brought it to the girls.	Marnie needed a prop and asked the teacher to help her. However, the three girls didn't seem to need more help as they were playing well without any other adult assistance.
Derek was in the dramatic play area with three other boys. The area was set up as a pizza restaurant. Each boy was playing on his own with no direct connections between them. One boy was at the cash register, two boys were making pizza, and Derek was writing on a pad.	Co-player: The teacher entered the play as a customer. As the customer, she asked Derek to take her order and tell the pizza makers what she wanted. She asked Derek to get the bill from the boy at the cash register and then she paid him.	The boys were playing, but not together. The teacher helped them make connections with each other so they could learn how to interact in their different roles and see how they fit together.
Maria, the teacher, watched several children enter her new dramatic play area, a doctor's office. They tried on the scrubs and laughed at the X-rays, but didn't adopt any roles.	Play Leader: The teacher plans to be in the doctor's office when the area opens. She plays a role, such as a patient or a doctor, and gives each child a role (nurse, doctor, receptionist, other patients). She withdraws when children are playing their roles.	By Maria's example, the children learn about the roles in a doctor's office and how the props are used. They learn vocabulary from their interactions with Maria. They gain confidence and are able to play without her involvement.
Abdul wasn't joining any play in the dramatic play area. He just stood at the side while others played. His teachers had never seen him play any role or even pretend with objects.	_____ _____ _____ _____ _____	_____ _____ _____ _____ _____
Honey was very shy and wouldn't play in any of the learning areas. She sat by herself at a table. Occasionally she would go to the water table, but if other children came over, she would leave again.	_____ _____ _____ _____ _____	_____ _____ _____ _____ _____

Time to Reflect

What was your experience with this exercise? What were your questions after completing it?

_____

_____

_____

_____

There is no definite right or wrong answer for these situations. You will be making a judgment based on your knowledge of the child, your goals, and your own comfort level. Sometimes you may try a role and find the child or children are not responding to it. If you have tried it for a time and they still are not responding, then you can try something else. Use the children's responses as your barometer.

Time to Reflect

Describe a time you joined in the play with the children in the dramatic play center. What role did you play? How did the children respond?

_____

_____

_____

_____

Your Comfort Level with Play

When you reflected on joining the play with children, you may remember feeling unsure of what you should be doing. Adults are accustomed to playing a leadership role in the classroom. When you are a co-player, you give up that role and ask children to be the leaders. When you engage in parallel play with a child, you are following the lead of the child. Sometimes when teachers describe playing with children, they tell us they feel self-conscious. Perhaps you feel a little embarrassed, especially if there are other adults in your learning environment. If you are able to put aside that embarrassment even for short periods, you may find it to be of great benefit to the children.

By playing a role in the play, you help children gain more skill and enrich their participation. They can expand cognitively, emotionally, and physically. They learn to express themselves and to plan ahead with other children. When you can play any adult role, from observer to play leader, you will be able to respond to the needs of the children. You will not be bound by your own discomfort; you will be making decisions based on your goals for the children.

Time to Reflect

How do you play as an adult in your life outside of the classroom?

_____

_____

_____

_____

How do you feel when you enter the play of a group of children? When are you most likely to enter the play? When are you least likely?

_____

_____

_____

_____

Look at your answers. Where would you place your comfort level with entering children's play and performing a role?

Very Comfortable   *Very Uncomfortable*

←————————————————————————————————→

What might you do to increase your comfort level with entering children's play?

_____

_____

_____

_____

Increasing Your Comfort Level

Increasing your comfort level so that playing with children feels natural is tricky. Some of us are shy and become very self-conscious playing like children. Others of us enter in with relish but forget to withdraw quickly when the children have the general idea of the play theme. You want to be able to enter play with children as well as observe because it gives you options. Your participation in play can help children understand the dramatic play theme, learn how to use the props, and experience how you model play skills. You base your decision on the children's needs. Here are some ways to increase your comfort level:

- Play with one child until you feel comfortable.
- Start with themes you are familiar with.
- Enter as a co-player and let the children tell you what to do in your role.
- Act out stories with the children such as "The Three Billy Goats Gruff" or "Goldilocks and the Three Bears."
- Do silly rhymes with the children to loosen your inhibition.

If you decide to take the role of the play leader, remember to step back to an observer or stage manager role when children are doing well together. When children control the play, they gain imagination, develop the ability to regulate their emotions, and feel empowered.

Completing the Planning Process

After you have chosen a focus area for the child, written your goal, planned an activity or strategy, and picked out your role, you are ready to fill out a planning form. Fill out the following planning form on your observed child. Include a strategy you will use during play and an activity or strategy you will use outside of play.

Planning Form

Child's name _____ Date _____

Goal (from chapter 6)

Who? _____

Does what? _____

Where? _____

How well or how often? _____

By when? _____

Activity during Play

What? _____

When? _____

Props or materials _____

Who will be involved? _____

My role _____

Reflection

Try the activity you planned. How did the activity go? Would you change it in any way?

_____

_____

_____

_____

Activity Outside of Play

What? _____

When? _____

Props or materials _____

Who will be involved? _____

Finding the time and energy to plan after long days with children can be easier said than done. However, once you have a focus and a goal, finding strategies to support that goal can give you new energy. Use your creativity and your knowledge of the child to find activities that will work. Observing how the child responds to your plan will give you the information you need to take the next step.

Time to Reflect

How did you experience the planning process? Would you change it in any way?

_____

_____

_____

_____

Implement your activity with the child for about a week. How did the child respond?

_____

_____

_____

_____

What did you learn about the child? How will this insight affect your next step?

_____

_____

_____

_____

CHAPTER 8 # Reflecting on Your Experience

Reflection is part of every step as you choose a child to observe, observe the child, complete the Play Checklist, and plan activities; it is especially important as you think about how your plan is working. Reflection is a chance for you to step back and consider how your plan went. You may have already adjusted or adapted the plan during your activity because the child was not responding as you expected. It is important, however, to spend time evaluating how the activity went after it is over. It can be helpful to reflect with others as well. They may remember details that you don't. You are often so busy carrying out the activity, you may miss important information. Ask yourself the following questions:

- Was the activity well prepared?

- How did the child respond?

- How did the other children respond?

- Were my interactions with the child appropriately matched to the child's needs?

- Did the activity catch the child's interest?

- What would I do again?

- What would I change?

- What would be the logical next step?

Content in this chapter connects with chapters 3 and 9 in *Play: The Pathway from Theory to Practice*.

Observe the child over the next few days to see if there is progress toward the goal. Continue to reinforce the goal in your interactions with the child during play. Reflect on the overall goal as well as the activity. Helping the child reach the goal you set requires continued planning and evaluation. It can be easy to become discouraged if the child is not making as much progress as you hoped. Learning new play skills takes time and practice. Look at the small ways you see progress and celebrate them.

Time to Reflect

How did you feel about your plan? What worked best? What do you want to do differently next time?

_____

_____

_____

_____

After reflecting on the goal and strategies for the child you observed, what are you planning on doing next?

_____

_____

_____

_____

Reflection Leads to Intentionality

Throughout this book and its companion you have been reflecting on what you are learning. Through reflection you gain a greater understanding of your skills, your learning environment, and what the children are learning. This depth of understanding enhances your work with children. Intentional teachers tend to help children make greater strides in meeting individual learning goals and reaching early learning standards.

Reflection can help you understand the responses of a child when you implement an activity. For example, your plan was to wash babies in the house area to help a child stay and play with other children for an extended amount of time. Instead, the child grabs all the dolls and tells other children to go away. What might have caused this behavior? It could be that the child could use a plan to help her play in a group and take turns. It could be, however, that she became anxious around the other children when they became excited about washing the babies and were crowding around. You can see you would plan very different activities the next time, depending on how you interpreted the child's actions. If the child needs to learn to take turns, you would devise several activities that encourage taking turns. If the child becomes anxious and agitated by the excitement of the children, you would need to structure the washing babies activity more. Perhaps you would limit the activity to a couple of children at a time.

Reflection also helps you decide which role you will take in play. When children are operating in the lower-level items on the Play Checklist, you will want to use roles that are more interactive and engaged in play. At other times children, especially when they are operating at the higher level on the checklist, need only a comment or suggestion to move them along. When you are engaged in play, reflect on the children's responses. If they are drawn to the area and engaged in play when you are playing a role, your involvement is helping them develop their play skills. If, however, they begin to wander off or look a little bored, you may have been too involved in the play and need to step back.

Reflection helps you evaluate the goal you have set for the child. If the strategies you have chosen to reach the goal are often unsuccessful, your goal may be too high. For example, you have written a goal for a child around solving problems. Right now the child uses force during conflicts. You decided you wanted the child to recall words or strategies to use when reminded. But even after you implemented your strategies, the child continued to hit or push when angry. Your strategy doesn't seem to be working, so you look at the checklist again. You see an item on the checklist right after "Uses force to solve problems" that states, "Seeks adult assistance." After reflecting on your goal and strategies, you decide to work with the child on seeking help from adults instead of hitting. After a couple of weeks, you see the child is looking for adults to help rather than hitting.

These examples show how reflection leads to intentionality. Intentional teaching is based on what you know about the child or children, what you want them to learn, and how best to engage them. Intentional teachers have knowledge of each of the domains of learning and know how to integrate them into their activities and lesson plans. When you teach intentionally, you have goals and defined outcomes you are working toward. Reflection helps you stay true to the children, yourself, and your teaching by providing a way to evaluate and modify your plans and strategies if needed. Reflection helps you:

- understand play as part of child development.

- set up and design your learning environment to encourage play.

- observe and assess children's play skills.

- plan goals and strategies.

- plan your role in play.

- evaluate what is working and what is not working about your plan.

- decide on next steps.

As an intentional teacher you are an active participant in the continuous cycle of improvement as you support a child in play. You are constantly in one of the following steps of the cycle:

- Observe and assess child's play skills

- Plan goals for the child

- Plan strategies

- Implement plan

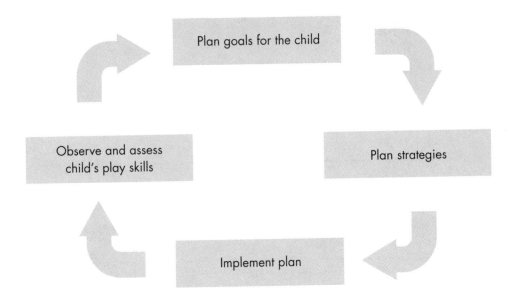

In each of these steps, you use your reflections to help you accurately assess the child, plan and implement the strategies, and evaluate how the plan is going. By paying attention to the continuous cycle of improvement you help children become more engaged and involved during play.

❋ Shelly was very concerned about one of the children in her group. Nadia hung around the edges of the house area but wouldn't enter the play. She didn't say much even when other children addressed her. Shelly decided to complete the Play Checklist for Nadia. When she did, she discovered that Nadia was having difficulty with sections 3.Verbalizations about the Play Scenario; 4. Verbal Communication during a Play Episode; and 7. Entrance into a Play Group.

Shelly decided to work on 7. Entrance into a Play Group because she thought that when Nadia was part of the group, she would join in. She used the strategies suggested by the checklist. However, on a number of occasions Nadia refused to enter the group and started going to another area of the room when Shelly tried to coach her. She observed Nadia at other times of the day as well and realized Nadia just wasn't talking much at any time. Shelly changed her plan. First she knew Nadia's family spoke another language at home, had just come to the country in the last year, and that this was Nadia's first school experience. Her parents had told staff that she could speak English. But Shelly wondered if Nadia's limited English was blocking her from playing with her peers. Shelly decided to work on language with Nadia. She used several language techniques, such as expanding Nadia's sentences and modeling language during play and at other times of the day as well. Nadia gradually started playing in the house area with one or two other children. She still didn't say much but did participate with gestures and short phrases.

Time to Reflect

Do you think Shelly is an intentional teacher? Why or why not?

_____

_____

_____

_____

How did reflection help Shelly be more responsive to the child's needs?

_____

_____

_____

_____

What do you do that defines you as an intentional teacher? Give an example from your work.

_____

_____

_____

_____

Children love to play, but it isn't always fun or easy. Children often need adult assistance to solve problems, find materials, and learn to use language to tell a story. This book and its companion, *When Play Isn't Fun: Helping Children Resolve Play Conflicts*, along with the book *Play: The Pathway from Theory to Practice*, have offered numerous suggestions, observation tools, and play strategies. Use them intentionally to help children grow in their play skills so they are more able to form friendships, pretend in play, and find the shared story. Through your observations, careful planning and implementation, responsive connections to children, and thoughtful reflections, you build on children's strengths and interests and give them expanded possibilities in play. You help children gain confidence and enthusiasm for play. You help them connect to other children and make friends. You are building a community in your learning environment where no one is excluded, children feel accepted, and play is at the center of the curriculum.

There have been a couple of occasions when I've been outside with my brothers' grandkids, and after a while they start imagining themselves in adult roles, imagining conversations and actions, much like I did as a four-year-old cowboy hero. So I think they have a natural tendency to have some imagined play. My own son, who grew up to become a computer whiz, used to stand at the kitchen table and make drawings, one after another, while singing a story, sort of a kitchen table artist opera. When he was four, he also dressed up in a straw cowboy hat, pulled on my size ten cowboy boots, and announced his new name was Carvalet the Cowboy. He was way ahead of me. I don't think I ever thought up a name for myself. —Steve M.

Children will always respond to curiosity . . . and play. There will always be successful teachers setting up creative and at times unorthodox play to provide new thinking and stimulation. —Sameerah

PLAY CHECKLIST

Child's Name: _____ Date: _____ Date of Birth: _____

Check the highest level skills you consistently observe:

*1. Pretending with Objects
- ❏ Does not use objects to pretend
- ❏ Uses real objects
- ❏ Substitutes objects for other objects
- ❏ Uses imaginary objects

*2. Role-Playing
- ❏ No role play
- ❏ Uses one sequence of play
- ❏ Combines sequences
- ❏ Uses verbal declaration (for example, "I'm a doctor")
- ❏ Imitates actions of role, including dress

*3. Verbalizations about the Play Scenario
- ❏ Does not use pretend words during play
- ❏ Uses words to describe substitute objects
- ❏ Uses words to describe imaginary objects and actions (for example, "I'm painting a house")
- ❏ Uses words to create a play scenario (for example, "Let's say we're being taken by a monster")

*4. Verbal Communication during a Play Episode
- ❏ Does not verbally communicate during play
- ❏ Talks during play only to self
- ❏ Talks only to adults in play
- ❏ Talks with peers in play by stepping outside of role (for example, "That's not how mothers hold their babies")
- ❏ Talks with peers from within role (for example, "Eat your dinner before your dad comes home")

*5. Persistence in Play
- ❏ Less than five minutes
- ❏ Six to nine minutes
- ❏ Ten minutes or longer

*6. Interactions
- ❏ Plays alone
- ❏ Plays only with adults
- ❏ Plays with one child, always the same person
- ❏ Plays with one child, can be different partners
- ❏ Can play with two or three children together

**7. Entrance into a Play Group
- ❏ Does not attempt to enter play group
- ❏ Uses force to enter play group
- ❏ Stands near group and watches
- ❏ Imitates behavior of group
- ❏ Makes comments related to play theme
- ❏ Gets attention of another child before commenting

8. Problem Solving
- ❏ Gives in during conflict
- ❏ Uses force to solve problems
- ❏ Seeks adult assistance
- ❏ Imitates verbal solutions or strategies provided by adults
- ❏ Recalls words or strategies to use when reminded
- ❏ Initiates use of words or strategies
- ❏ Accepts reasonable compromises

9. Turn Taking
- ❏ Refuses to take turns
- ❏ Leaves toys, then protests when others pick them up
- ❏ Takes turns if arranged and directed by an adult
- ❏ Asks for turn, does not wait for a response
- ❏ Gives up toy easily if done with it
- ❏ Gives up toy if another child asks for it
- ❏ Proposes turn taking, will take and give turns

10. Support of Peers
- ❏ Shows no interest in peers
- ❏ Directs attention to distress of peers
- ❏ Shows empathy or offers help
- ❏ Offers and takes suggestions of peers at times
- ❏ Encourages or praises peers

Note: The developmental progression outlined in each segment of the Play Checklist can be used as a guideline when assessing most children's development. However, not all children will go through the same steps in development nor through the same developmental sequence.

* Sara Smilansky. 1968. *The Effects of Sociodramatic Play on Disadvantaged Preschool Children.* New York: Wiley.

** Nancy Hazen, Betty Black, and Faye Fleming-Johnson. 1984. Social Acceptance: Strategies Children Use and How Teachers Can Help Children Learn Them. *Young Children* 39: 26–36.